Praise for

As an industry insider, I highly re[...] comprehensive guide to writing one of the most popular genres today. [...] emerging screenwriter is lucky to have the benefit of Muir's experience and advice.

> DARIA ELLERMAN, Editor (*Meditation Park, Virgin River*)

Roslyn Muir's *Writing a TV Movie* is a must-read for anyone looking to write their first MOW. With our busy lives the short, easy-to-read chapters makes absorbing the material super easy. And Muir covers everything from the different types of genres to writing a synopsis to breaking down the full script and then how to pitch it. She really takes you from how to get an idea to how to make a sale! And she asks some of North America's top screenwriters to share their best tips for breaking in — honestly, that alone is a reason to buy this book.

> HEATHER HAWTHORN DOYLE, Director
> (*A Little Daytime Drama, A Godwink Christmas*)

An invaluable analysis of TV movie structure.

> PEGGY THOMPSON, Screenwriter/Co-Producer
> (*Better Than Chocolate, The Lotus Eaters*)

Roslyn Muir has written a must-read primer — it's a terrific guide to writing for television movies in North America, with solid, practical advice for beginners.

> ALEXANDRA RAFFÉ, Producer (*Kim's Convenience, Strays*)

If you're a writer who is interested in breaking into TV movie writing, this is the indispensable guide for you. Muir breaks down the structure of the genre in a way that is both practical and entertaining. As a television and feature film screenwriter who has worked in a number of structures, I found this guide so helpful. Muir has done the research, so you don't have to! Highly recommended, for both novices and professionals alike.

> KAREN LAM, Screenwriter and Director
> (*The Curse of Willow Song, Van Helsing*)

A seasoned screenwriter, Muir offers up her expertise and real-world experience making this a must-have book for writers of all levels and interests. This informative and entertaining book is an excellent resource for new screenwriters wanting to break into the film and TV industry. Highly recommend!

> AVI FEDERGREEN, President/Producer, Federgreen Entertainment Inc.

Writing a TV Movie: An Insider's Guide to Launching a Screenwriting Career is an invaluable resource for any aspiring screenwriter looking to break into the industry or an emerging one looking to strengthen their craft and/or advance their career. Roslyn Muir provides a clear, concise blueprint on how to master the highly structured TV movie format, from which creativity is free to blossom, but also provides engaging, realistic tips and insights on how to get your work out there, so that your career can blossom, too!
>> Rachelle Chartrand, Producer (*Chained, Downloaded*)

If you want to break into writing TV movies, this book is a MUST read. Muir gives you a clear, manageable format for writing your movie and walks you through every step to getting your script on the screen. It has not only helped me as a writer but also as an actor by helping me understand why the scene is in the movie. Highly recommend this book!
>> Tammy Gillis, Actress and Executive Producer (*Riverfront Romance, Siren*)

A one-of-a-kind comprehensive guide to writing and selling a TV movie. Learn the detailed requirements for story, genre, structure, and character development and you are off to the races to become a screenwriter.
>> Penelope Buitenhuis, Screenwriter and Director (*Death of a Vegas Showgirl, Mistress Hunter*)

Having worked with Roslyn to create *Stranger in the House*, indeed, a television movie, I can attest to the fact that she's extremely knowledgeable on the subject. If you'd like to learn the 'ins and outs' of how to put a contemporary television movie screenplay together, this book should be of enormous benefit to you.
>> Allan Harmon, Director of over 20 Television Movies

An essential and immensely readable guide for any writer — novice or experienced — wanting to break into the TV Movie industry.
>> Sharon McGowan, Producer and Associate Professor, UBC School of Creative Writing and UBC Film Production Program

WRITING A TV MOVIE

An Insider's Guide
to Launching a
Screenwriting Career

WRITING A TV MOVIE

An Insider's Guide to Launching a Screenwriting Career

ROSLYN MUIR

THREE OCEAN PRESS

Copyright © 2021 Roslyn Muir

All rights reserved. No part of this publication may be reproduced, stored in a retrieval system, or transmitted, in any form or by any means, electronic, mechanical, photocopying, recording, or otherwise, without prior written permission of the publisher.

Library and Archives Canada Cataloguing in Publication

Title: Writing a TV movie : an insider's guide to launching a screenwriting career / Roslyn Muir.
Other titles: Writing a television movie
Names: Muir, Roslyn, author.
Description: Includes bibliographical references.
Identifiers: Canadiana (print) 20210330147 | Canadiana (ebook) 20210330155 | ISBN 9781988915364 (softcover) | ISBN 9781988915371 (EPUB)
Subjects: LCSH: Made-for-TV movies—Authorship—Handbooks, manuals, etc. | LCGFT: Handbooks and manuals.
Classification: LCC PN1992.7 .M85 2021 | DDC 808/.066791—dc23

Editors: Erin Linn McMullan & Kyle Hawke
Proofreader: Carol Hamshaw
Book Designer: PJ Perdue
Cover Designer: Amanda Walker PA & Design Services
Author Photo: Roslyn Muir

Three Ocean Press
8168 Riel Place
Vancouver, BC, V5S 4B3
778.321.0636
info@threeoceanpress.com
www.threeoceanpress.com

First publication, November 2021

*To all the screenwriters
with their overflowing swear jars:
you got this.*

Acknowledgements

The saying "it takes a village" has never been more appropriate than in the creation of this book — so many people have helped me by giving feedback and support. The stars aligned when I was referred to publisher Kyle Hawke and Three Ocean Press. Working with Kyle has been a super experience and I greatly admire anyone who can take my random musings and polish it up for public consumption. His knowledge and rigor has been the fuel I needed to propel me to completion on this project. I'm also forever indebted to my amazing friend and developmental editor who encouraged me to dig deeper into the text, Erin Linn McMullan, who works from Tofino, BC, within the traditional Ha-houthlee and Tribal Parks of the Tla-o-qui-aht First Nation.

I'm also thrilled that the screenwriters I interviewed for the book took time out of their busy days to impart such wonderful, writerly advice. A huge thanks to Melissa Cassera, Carley Smale, Kraig Wenman, Kelly Peters, Amy Taylor, and Keith Shaw — who also gave me my first break writing MOWs and mentored me through it all. I'm very grateful for my screenwriter friends who sat through early versions of the book and asked all the right questions: Michelle McLean, Vesta Giles, Heather Hewitt, Olivia Rendall, Tyquira Dixon-Traer, and Jude Klassen. Thank you for all your insights and feedback.

PART ONE

The TV movie genre and its place in the North American entertainment industry

Contents

Acknowledgements ix

Introduction xiii

PART ONE
The TV movie genre and its place in the North American entertainment industry 1

    What are TV movies? 3

    Who makes TV movies? 9

    What are the genre rules for these networks? 13

PART TWO
How to create a TV movie screenplay 19

    How to write a TV movie 21

    The nine-act structure 31

    The thriller plot 37

    The rom-com plot 45

    Writing the TV movie script 53

PART THREE
Pitching your project to producers and next steps 61

    How to find producers to pitch to 63

    Making the sale 69

    Launching a screenwriting career 73

Resources 77

    Question & Answer 79

    Glossary 89

    Recommended reading 91

    Websites 91

About the Author 93

Introduction

As storytellers, we aren't bound by genre — screenwriters just want to tell their stories and move an audience in some way. Whether it be through traditional film and television or through a short film on the internet, the goal is always the same. Our stories need to be told.

I've been a screenwriter for over a decade and have been fortunate to make a steady career out of it. Long before I had any produced writing credits, I was advised by a mentor to write a TV movie. She assured me that getting a major credit would lead to other work. And she was right.

At the time, I was consumed with writing feature film scripts and didn't know anything about TV movies. I scoured the internet for information but there were few resources for writing this specialized genre. I had to watch a slew of movies, study them, and figure it out for myself. But I was stabbing in the dark and wasted a lot of time.

After having several TV movies produced, I finally felt like I got it. Then the networks changed the act structure of TV movies from seven to nine and I had to relearn the structure requirements.

Who is this book for?

I'm writing this book to give new, aspiring, and experienced screenwriters a way to write a popular genre without reinventing the wheel. I aim to demystify the process of writing the TV movie and up your chances of becoming a credited writer. Even if you've never considered writing in this genre, you can still add a TV movie script sample to your writing toolbox to show your versatility.

TV movies are popular all around the world. My movies have been produced for the Canadian, US, and international markets; they have been filmed in the US and Canada. Those of us writing TV movies might all be writing for the same markets, but those markets are hungry ones: Hallmark, Lifetime, and streamers like Netflix. There's never been a better time to write a TV movie and get it produced!

What will you learn?

This book is laid out in three parts:

- **Part One** introduces the reader to the TV movie genre and its place in the North American entertainment industry.

- **Part Two** gives detailed instructions to help you create a TV movie screenplay.

- **Part Three** reveals how to pitch your project to producers and launch your screenwriting career.

If you're unfamiliar with any of the screenwriting terms I've mentioned throughout the book, check the Glossary at the back.

There's a special treat for writers in the Resources section. I was thrilled to interview several successful TV movie screenwriters, who've shared some great advice. In the Q&A you'll find: Melissa Cassera, who wrote the *Obsession* thriller trilogy (Lifetime); Carley Smale, who wrote *Christmas Pen Pals* (Lifetime); Kraig Wenman, who wrote *Secret Obsession* (Netflix); Keith Shaw, who wrote *Maternal Instinct* (Lifetime); and the writing team of Kelly Peters and Amy Taylor, who together created *A Taste of Christmas* (Lifetime).

All advice given here is based on my experiences in the film and TV industry and primarily pertains to the North American market. The big three producers of TV movies — Hallmark, Lifetime, and Netflix — are my reference points, but there are many other networks and streamers who are now producing them.

- You have great film and TV samples.
- You've even interned on a series or been a production assistant.

But why can't you break through?

If you check IMDb.com and look up your favorite screenwriters or showrunners, you'll see that a lot of them started at the bottom. They will have credits in other departments. They may have worked in other genres — factual, documentary, or children's entertainment. Of course, not all of them wrote TV movies, but they all started someplace that gave them an edge: a professional credit.

As a new writer, getting a credit on IMDb is a must. IMDb is the industry go-to for checking on someone's credentials and experience level. Producers use it all the time.

Writing a TV movie and getting it produced is a great way to kickstart your career. Technically, it's a TV credit. But since it's also a movie, you can spin it to your advantage when pitching other projects.

The top TV movie genres

The top TV movie genres are:
- Romantic comedy *a.k.a.* rom-com
- Thriller
- Ripped from the headlines *a.k.a.* based on true stories

Of course, there are other TV movie genres like action and horror that are popular too, but fewer of these movies are made.

Know your audience

If you're writing for Lifetime, Hallmark, or Netflix, then your audience is women!

The key audience demographics for Hallmark and Lifetime are women 25–54 and women 18+, respectively. Both channels have a huge viewership comprised of mostly women who love thrillers and rom-coms.

Women of all ages watch these movies. Back in the day, my mom watched them. For fun, search online for some of the older TV movies from the 1970s. We've come a long way, baby!

Where to find TV movies

As a screenwriter, you need to invest in your career and know the markets. The best way to do that is to watch everything. If you want to write TV movies, in the thriller-for-women genre. These aren't hardcore crime dramas. Known as "woman-in-peril" thrillers, they offer a softer, bloodless two hours of entertainment. Mostly whodunits, they focus on the female protagonist and their need to be heard and to rescue themselves.

The need for entertaining content

All genres of TV movies aim to entertain. Channels like Hallmark and Lifetime work on the idea of higher volume vs. higher budget experience. But they're also giving their viewers what they demand: more light, easy-to-watch content that they can escape into.

Why write TV movies?

Most of us screenwriters are working on our award speeches. So why write TV movies if you really want to write film and series TV?

- Writing a TV movie is a good way to get established as a screenwriter.
- Getting that elusive first long-form credit can propel your screenwriting career into the professional realm.
- Producers are always looking for content and, in a relatively short timeframe, you can get a professional writing credit.
- The development and production time of a TV movie is much quicker than a TV series or a feature film.

While it's not particularly easy to get a TV movie made, it is most definitely easier than completing a feature film or TV series. Producers and networks are more willing to take a chance on a *new* screenwriter. Screenwriters with one or two produced TV movies tend to move on to other, more lucrative genres, so producers are always looking for writers.

The most difficult aspect of being a screenwriter is breaking into the business. Often, new screenwriters are in that early career catch-22. You can't get any work because you don't have a major credit. You can't get a major credit because you don't have any work.

Believe me, many writers have been in the same predicament at the start of their careers:

- You've been through a good writing program or film school.
- You've come out of the gate with a short film that did well on the festival circuit.
- You've won a screenplay contest or placed high.

Why are TV movies so popular?

TV movies are entertainment. In a busy world where most of us are bombarded by social media, work, and family responsibilities, two hours of familiar entertainment can be a comfort.

The decline of TV soap operas

The soap opera is a daily, serialized one-hour drama that viewers, primarily women, used to flock to. Soaps like *Days of Our Lives*, *General Hospital*, and *The Young and the Restless* all had a fervent viewer base that has lessened over time.

These shows started in the 1950s and '60s when TV networks realized they had a captive audience in housewives — and could market products to them. This dedicated group of female viewers became hooked on the daily dose of drama. But decades later, as economies changed and more and more women entered the workforce, the popularity of soap operas waned. Networks picked up the slack and offered the TV movie as a substitute.

Dedicated TV channels like Lifetime and Hallmark with an equally dedicated audience

Hallmark is synonymous with the TV movie.

They are renowned for their entertaining, seasonal movies and are dedicated to delivering hundreds of movies a year to their audience. Lifetime was one of the first dedicated TV channels to present TV movies to a specific audience. Both channels have a primarily female viewership that can reach two to three million views per movie.

The uptick in streamers like Netflix and a wider, more diverse audience

Streamers like Netflix are reaching a more diverse audience. While they do not have the TV commercials that these movies were originally designed for, they still have the same structure and appeal to a wide audience.

The popularity of uplifting content like rom-coms

Romance is hot! Since film was invented, the romance genre has ebbed and flowed in popularity but has seen a huge revival because of channels like Hallmark that are solely dedicated to love.

The popularity of crime drama and ripped-from-the-headlines stories

The crime and thriller genres are huge in entertainment and books. Who doesn't love a murder mystery or gory thriller? Lifetime TV has been a leader

CHAPTER ONE

What are TV movies?

Christmas Unwrapped. Married at First Sight. You Had Me at Aloha. What do all these titles have in common? They're all TV movies.

The TV movie, also called movie-of-the-week or MOW, is a form unto itself and the workhorse of the entertainment industry. It's a movie that's more TV than film since it adheres to a structure initially created around TV commercial breaks.

Back in the 1960s and '70s, these movies were literally programmed and promoted on TV networks as the "Movie of the Week," thus the name. Of course, now that we live in a universe of endless TV channels and streamers, the moniker may seem outdated, but the film and TV industry still uses it to identify the type of project it is. TV professionals use *MOW* or *TV movie* to identify these genres, with the terms interchangeable.

The TV movie is presented as a two-hour film but structured like a TV episode, using nine acts in order to support as many TV commercial breaks as possible.

In the past, the TV movie was synonymous with cheesy, cheap production values and thin plotlines. Times have changed and while cheesy, cheap, thin TV movies may still abound, there are also big-budget versions with popular actors in key roles. As the audience has grown and evolved, so too has the TV movie.

They are still called TV movies because the most popular networks for these movies — Hallmark and Lifetime — continue to broadcast on regular TV. These movies were never written for a theatrical release; they're specifically written for the small screen.

then you need to watch them to understand your target audience and the tone of the movie.

If you don't have a subscription to Hallmark, Lifetime, or Netflix, you can find recent TV movies on YouTube. However, the older movies will have a different six- or seven-act structure than is used today. Almost every streamer will give you a one-month free subscription. You can also buy or rent movies from your favorite online retailer.

While I'll give you genre specifics shortly, doing a bit of research first will help you define the type of TV movie you want to write. The top two genres are thriller and rom-com. Start there.

> ### Research Assignment
> - Watch three movies from each genre.
> - Study them: note how the genre works. What are the parameters, the must-haves of the genre? How many love interests in a rom-com? How many suspects in a thriller?
> - Compare them. Which movies did you like best and why?
> - What was it about one of them that elevated the story above others?
> - When you find some movies that you enjoy and are well-crafted, note the production company and producer names in the credits.
> - Create a spreadsheet of movie titles, the year they came out, and their producers.
> - Now watch three more movies in each genre!

If you've watched six or more TV movies, that should give you a good sense of which genre you prefer. But six producers' names are not much to go on. Head over to the Hallmark and Lifetime websites and get the names of their new titles. Search these titles on IMDb.com and continue to add the producer names to your list. Find out what else they have produced and make note of it. All this information will be useful in Part Three.

This research is imperative to knowing which genre you want to write and finding producers to pitch to. Spoiler alert: you will have to watch more TV movies!

Yes, some producers may be too big to find contact information for, but often you can find that newer producer who is hungry for ideas.

The regular IMDb won't have contact information for these producers. You will need IMDbPro. It's not free — you will have to purchase a subscription.

But they often have a 30-day free trial. If you're on a budget, use this option, but wait until you're ready to pitch.

There's also LinkedIn. There, you can find links to production company websites and contact information for producers.

> **NOTE**
> I will discuss how to find producers who make this content in Part Three. But here's a warning up front — do not attempt to pitch directly to Hallmark, Lifetime, Netflix, or other networks. They will not take pitches from writers. They generally only deal with experienced distributors and producers. When researching, you may notice networks and production companies specifying "No unsolicited submissions" on their website and contact pages. This means you may only send submissions through a recognized agent or entertainment lawyer. This is why your research is so important — you must find the producers who make TV movies and pitch to them.

Do all your research first and create a big list of producers. This list is very important and something I cannot create for you. Each of you lives in a different area of the world and has access to different markets. Regardless of where you live, you need to build your contact base — and it takes time, so start now!

CHAPTER TWO

Who makes TV movies?

As you try to decide which genre is best for you, studying the actual streamers and networks will give you a better sense of what they're looking for.

> **NOTE**
> The networks and streamers are not necessarily the producers of the movie — they may have acquired (bought) them after they were created.

Screenwriting is an odd collaboration between art and commerce. Your indie feature film skews more in the art vein. Your slick TV series is a good combination of art and commerce. The TV movie is primarily commerce. Sure, they're created with an imagination, but they are specifically entertainment for a mass market. Some people view the genre as cookie-cutter or factory writing, but it also allows for creativity and a way into a lucrative career. And they're fun to write!

Always research your target network. Do not pitch genres that they don't normally produce. You won't see supernatural or sci-fi stories on Hallmark. You won't see rip-roaring comedies on Lifetime.

The primary markets for TV movies are Lifetime, Hallmark, and Netflix because they are making the most content.

Lifetime

The Lifetime Movie Network produces thrillers and darker fare. Their movies are dramatic, suspenseful, but always have a happy, satisfying ending. Ripped-from-the-headlines stories are also popular.

This channel primarily has female-driven TV movies called "woman-in-peril" stories. The protagonist is smart, modern, and active. She's 26–34, and has a good, professional job. She's very capable and the viewer wants to be her. Ultimately, the viewer lives vicariously through her.

The Lifetime thriller has been a staple for the network for years now. And they're in big demand by the viewer. Thus, scripts in this genre of TV movie are in big demand by producers. Lifetime puts all this programming aside at Christmas and plays only holiday movies, which they also produce. In fact, Lifetime produced thirty Christmas-themed rom-coms alone in 2020.

The Lifetime TV channel has a variety of dramatic series as well as reality series. There is also the Lifetime Movie Club — a streaming service with no commercials. It offers all the movies you can handle, anytime you want them.

Hallmark

Hallmark is generally known for its soft dramas and seasonal romantic comedies. Their message is love, optimism, and positivity. They pretty much invented the Christmas-themed rom-com — their highest-watched genre. In 2020, they produced a record forty Christmas movies. These TV movies consistently hit three to four million viewers — each. Their December movies easily top fifty million views. Hallmark has a seriously dedicated audience!

The G-rated holiday TV movies are "light" love stories set around Christmas — but not the super-religious part of Christmas. It's more like the family values of the season: let's be together at Christmas — and make cookies, of course! The holiday season has become the most romantic of the year.

Hallmark likes other seasonal fare as well:
- spring fling
- summer romance
- harvest/fall stories (but no Hallowe'en settings)

It also has sub-genres of the rom-com:
- princess stories — (yes, you read that right. There's a slew of royal-themed romances to choose from)
- Valentine's Day (these come second to Christmas movies)
- travel stories (who doesn't want to fall in love on vacay?)
- dramatic romances (more rom than com)

This channel primarily has female-driven TV movies. Like Lifetime, the protagonist is also smart, modern, and active, 26–34, with a good, professional job. The viewer lives vicariously through her romance. Hallmark is also open to stories about older women and to stories that incorporate diversity and cultural elements.

Hallmark has a streaming service, Hallmark Movies Now, and has branched out to dramatic TV series on Hallmark's Movies and Mysteries channel. These popular, serial shows are classed as "cozy mysteries" and run two hours — so technically, each episode is a TV movie.

Some examples:
- *Aurora Teagarden Mysteries*
- *Picture Perfect Mysteries*
- *Matchmaker Mysteries*
- *The Gourmet Detective*

This channel converts to all-Christmas fare in December.

Netflix

Netflix is fairly new in the TV movie arena. In the past, they have acquired TV movies from other networks, but are now heavily invested in the Netflix Original Movie. Netflix is a streamer, not a TV channel, and is subscription-based. This means that it's user-pay and there are no TV commercials. So, the term *TV movie* is used loosely here when talking about Netflix fare, but it's still a movie that wasn't released theatrically. The genre and content of these movies make them similar because they also use a multi-act structure.

The primary difference between Netflix and the networks is that they seem to have more contemporary stories and higher budgets. Their stories take more risks, have more romance and diversity, and have younger main characters.

Other places to find TV movies

Of course, other networks and streamers carry original TV movies. More and more networks are capitalizing on the popularity of this genre, which means more opportunities for writers! (This list is not exhaustive.)

UpTV is a cable network that is often bundled on streamers and networks. They create original programming that includes positive stories, rom-com, and faith-based TV movies. UpTV has annual "Merry Movie Christmas" holiday programming that runs from early November through the holiday season.

If you like genres like creature features, disaster, and sci-fi, then you can write stories for SYFY. Technically, many of them are TV movies because they adhere to the multi-act structure and wouldn't get a theatrical release like bigger budget fare. SYFY had a huge hit with the *Sharknado* series of movies, but soon reined in the number of movies they were making. SYFY even does Christmas-themed TV movies like *Toys of Terror* and *Letters to Satan Claus*.

Other networks and streamers like Disney Plus, ION Television, OWN, Fox, CBS, and the Paramount Movie Network are also producing TV movies.

Hallmark, Lifetime, and Netflix are the best reference points because they are the biggest producers of TV movies.

CHAPTER THREE

What are the genre rules for these networks?

Hopefully, by this point you're becoming familiar with the parameters of TV movie genres. Each network has its own rules around the genre, but these rules are constantly changing.

The Hallmark rom-com

In the past, Hallmark would not allow characters who were divorced, single parents, non-white, or LGBTQIA+. All that has changed, though progress may seem slow. This new, inclusive approach reveals that their audience is changing.

In 2020, Hallmark released the LGBTQIA+ movie, *The Christmas House*, which centers on a gay male couple about to adopt their first baby. Will the baby arrive by Christmas and ensure everyone's happiness?

Hallmark does still have some rules around marriage to be aware of. It's acceptable if your characters are recently widowed or divorced, just don't focus on it or make it part of the plot. Treat it as a backstory for their characters. Never have characters with messy divorces or creepy ex-husbands — save that for Lifetime.

Morally, the characters remain squeaky clean. Absolutely no sex or nudity, and no swearing! No premarital sex, unless the character was previously married. Most couples in Hallmark rom-coms will not get past the first kiss!

The protagonist, or main character, is almost always a woman. Of course, there are always exceptions to every rule. Hallmark is now open to lesbian and gay romance, and male protagonists are allowed. The movie, *The Christmas Train*, adapted from a book, features a male protagonist.

If you're writing rom-coms, your story should always focus on the main couple, the lovebirds, and how they make the audience feel and care. What are they missing in life? Why do they need each other? Give them equal screen time. Like in any rom-com movie, you always need the "meet-cute," that moment of spark between the main couple.

Simplify your story. It doesn't have to be complicated. It's the classic girl-meets-boy trope. Girl meets Boy. Girl is not sure if she wants or deserves Boy. But Girl falls in love with Boy anyway. This trope is true for Girl meets Girl and Boy meets Boy stories too. Although there are few male protagonists in these rom-coms, Boy meets Girl is also acceptable.

Go for the *aww!* feeling. Make sure there's a cute factor. It's entertainment! Make sure your character's attributes and traits are positive — no slobs or drunks! Their character traits must be integral to the story. Give your characters successful professions. The audience wants to live vicariously through your characters and experience new things, so they should be appealing.

Your protagonist needs a confidante or best friend. This character is always a bit quirky and comedic. Ditto the love interest — give him or her a bestie. These stories are dialogue-driven, so the protagonist depends on the best friend as a sounding board and device to reveal her feelings.

Multi-age characters are useful and expected: the mentor, wise parents or a meddling aunt, the caring/demanding boss, the elderly mayor, the young assistant, the matchmaker. Most of these stories don't feature children in big roles, but they are often featured in Christmas-themed movies.

The conflict in your story should be manageable. In a rom-com, it's always that push-pull energy between the protagonist and the love interest. Will they or won't they fall in love?

Hallmark movies are full of tropes: commonly recurring plot devices and clichés. Try to avoid them or play with them and use them for comedic effect. You can also put your own unique twist on these old stories.

Common Hallmark tropes (this list is not exhaustive):
- City girl goes back to her hometown to sell the farm but ends up falling for the farmer.
- City girl can't find love, so a friend matches her up with small-town boy. Love ensues.
- City girl accidentally dates a prince, and they fall in love. Oops!

- City girl can't go home for Christmas without a boyfriend, so she asks her best male friend to pretend they're in love. Romance ensues.
- City girl doesn't believe in the magic of Christmas and meets hot Santa. Romance ensues.

Don't be afraid to have those big moments and scenes: the romantic Valentine's dance, the busy Fall Fair, the elegant Cinderella Ball.

In Christmas-themed movies, you will need the Christmas Eve dinner, Christmas Day dinner, and any kind of Christmassy events like ice skating, gift shopping, attending a winter fair or carnival, making Christmas cookies, wrapping presents, decorating the tree, or a special family tradition or event.

Avoid things like tobogganing, skiing, or snowball fights. These movies are often shot in the summer — on the Prairies! Faux snow is expensive. Ice skating is a good winter activity that can be done in most seasons. However, if a producer has the budget and asks you to put in a skiing scene — go for it!

No matter what the season, rom-coms are primarily romances set against the backdrop of a holiday season. So, make sure your A-Plot is all about LOVE.

How much romance does your rom-com need?

> ROM-COM PLOTLINES
> A-PLOT — Love Story, 75%
> B-PLOT — Protagonist personal/career issues, 20%
> C-PLOT — Holiday season problem, 5%

The Lifetime thriller

The suspenseful thriller plot is a solid mystery — usually a murder — that needs to be solved by the protagonist. And she must succeed in her quest for the truth. She must solve the mystery and save herself from danger in the end. Yes, she will have ally characters, but she must go from danger to success. She's the 'woman-in-peril'!

The antagonist will bait, elude, and chase the protagonist, making sure she's always in danger. The antagonist is often someone close to her: the new boyfriend, the new husband, the conniving boss, the new best friend, the mentor, etc. The conflict between these two characters must be palpable and drive the story.

The protagonist is almost always in the dark about the killer's identity, but the audience can be privy to it. These stories must leave the viewers on the edge of their seats, but not be too thrilling, so go minimal on the blood. When a victim is killed, we need to know the method, but we don't usually see the gory details on screen.

The TV movie thriller often centers around the protagonist's family, or work family, so include them as secondary characters. Give her a friend and confidante. Give her a good profession that often relates to the crime she's trying to solve. She usually has a romantic partner — boyfriend or husband — but can also be single. So far, I haven't seen any LGBTQIA+ stories in the Lifetime thriller, but I'm sure they're in the works.

Even though it's a thriller, you can have a minor love interest in the story — the C-Plot — especially if our protagonist's spouse is the guilty party. The love interest is often the handsome cop who helps the protagonist, the sexy lawyer who may be a suspect, or the dependable family doctor who she goes to for advice. Often, this love story is just hinted at and not acted upon until the crime is resolved.

The audience needs to have a happily ever after. Even if it's just implied that they'll get together at the end of the story, it leaves the protagonist (and the audience) with a sense of hope after the thrilling, life-altering conclusion to the story.

There are always exceptions to the rule, especially with ripped-from-the-headlines stories — which generally stick to the truth.

This woman-in-peril genre has many tropes, often recycled and upcycled for today's audience. You can take any story type on this list and give it a creative spin.

Here are some thriller tropes:
- The woman who marries a killer.
- The woman who's wrongly accused of murder.
- The woman whose husband has faked his death.
- The woman who's stalked.
- The woman who hires the killer babysitter/nanny/caregiver.

There is also a popular teen protagonist wave of thrillers and tropes:
- The teen who is on the run.
- The teen cheerleader who's in danger.
- The teen who discovers her parents aren't who they say they are.
- The teen who is abducted/trapped/stalked.
- The teen who knows her stepfather is a killer.
- The teen who is pregnant or has a drug problem.

The cool thing about Lifetime is that they aren't afraid of current issues. While they do use tropes, they also have great original content and true, ripped-from-the-headlines stories. They explore difficult issues like drugs and addictions, rape and assault, abduction, and mental health problems. They have also made a point to involve the real victims and let them tell their stories. *I Was Lorena Bobbitt* is a good example of this and even includes narration by the real Lorena Bobbitt.

This genre of TV movie, while still thrillers, will not necessarily adhere to the rules. The story will dictate the content — protagonist age, class, and circumstances — but it will adhere to the TV movie structure.

How much thrill in your thriller?

The TV movie thriller is primarily a mystery.

> **THRILLER PLOTLINES**
> A-PLOT — Protagonist solves the mystery, 75%
> B-PLOT — Protagonist personal/relationship issues, 20%
> C-PLOT —Love story, 5%

The Lifetime rom-com

Long a dramatic network, Lifetime has become Hallmark's biggest competitor for the holiday rom-com viewer and was the first to have a same-sex kiss in their holiday fare. But, like Hallmark, their holiday movies still hit all the same tropes and ring familiar tones, so all the same rules apply.

Netflix

Netflix has consistently offered a variety of thriller and holiday-themed rom-com TV movies that at one point were mostly acquired from other networks like Hallmark and Lifetime. But they are now committed to producing their own TV movies in both genres.

They still want the same movies as Lifetime and Hallmark, but with a more contemporary spin. Netflix has much edgier content and bigger stars in their movies, and although the structure is mostly the same, they are more like feature films than TV movies. They seem to be keeping the content and multi-act structure of these much-loved TV movies but presenting them as films.

While they don't have a specific list of attributes for their TV movies, they do want diverse casting and stories. Netflix has just announced a gay Christmas rom-com, *Single All the Way*. They also look for more unique settings: *Falling Inn Love* sees a woman win a house and head to New Zealand where she also finds love. The armchair traveler in me loved this one!

PART TWO

How to create a TV movie screenplay

CHAPTER FOUR
How to write a TV movie

This book is written with the assumption that you already know the general structure and formatting of a screenplay. If you've never written any kind of screenplay before, you may want to head to the Resources page and check out a couple of books mentioned there. Take a screenwriting class, head online, and download some scripts too.

In order to pitch and work with a producer, you will need most if not all of the materials listed here:

- Logline
- Synopsis
- Outline
- Treatment
- Script

It may seem like a lot, but it's not wasted time and energy. I recommend creating all of these materials before you even start writing the script. Not all producers will ask for each and every element, but I have written and used all of them. I'm big on structure and doing as much pre-writing as possible before tackling the script. Trust me — it makes the process easier. Nailing down these elements gives you the structure to hang your story on.

If you don't have any professional screenwriting credits (i.e., nothing listed on IMDb), then you will need to write the script — called a *spec* script. The spec script means that you have written it as a sample, on speculation that you will sell it. (In TV series writing, a spec has a different meaning:

it means you have written an episode of an existing show.) Initially, it may seem like unpaid work, but besides being an investment in your career — you will hopefully sell it. You can also use it as a writing sample that showcases your abilities.

Producers usually don't want to develop a writer's *idea*: they want the script written up front. However, if you do have professional credits on IMDb, then you can most likely pitch a logline and synopsis to producers without writing the script. That's because an experienced writer with credits has a track record of delivering the script and a producer will be more confident investing in you as a writer.

Even so, most producers will prefer the finished script. They make these movies quickly and some production companies are filming more than a dozen per year. If you haven't written a TV movie before, it's highly recommended to write the script first. It will give you a chance to practice writing in the challenging nine-act structure and decide if this genre is for you.

Start with an idea

Like any script you create, it all starts with a great concept. One way to create more ideas is to challenge yourself daily and keep a notebook of ideas for future use. If you like, start with one of the tropes from the lists in the previous chapter and tell an old story with your own creative twist on it.

> **TIP**
> Write three TV movie ideas per day for one week — then increase it to five ideas per day. It's tough at first, but after a few weeks you will find that your mind is adapting and churning out ideas.

Choose a genre

What genre of TV movie are you attracted to? It helps to write in a genre that you like and would watch. If you're used to writing drama, you may want to go for the thriller. If you're a comedy writer, try the rom-com.

Then, pick a subgenre. If you picked rom-com, then decide if you want to do a Christmas-themed story or maybe a Valentine's story (both are in big demand). It's your choice. I try not to force a story.

I go with whichever idea will excite me long enough to get through the script phase. Although I've written a few rom-com scripts for practice, all my produced movies are thrillers. I love thrillers!

What about true stories?

If you have a true, ripped-from-the-headlines story that you would like to write, you first have to secure the rights to the story. These are called life rights. That means that the person involved in the story must give you permission to use their name and story in your movie. If your subject is deceased, you will still need to seek out the family of that person and make sure you have permission to write about them. Get it in writing.

Finding a true story in the media is usually not so difficult. But, by the time the story has hit the big news outlets, it's probably too late to secure the rights. I recommend looking in local newspapers and media outlets for stories. You must find that balance of notoriety vs. interest, and the story must be unique and have legs.

If you do have an interesting real-life story, and you haven't written a TV movie before, you can still pitch it as a concept. Find a producer who has done these ripped-from-the-headlines stories before. When producers have success in one genre, they're more likely to continue making movies in that genre.

It's all about access. How to get the rights? If it's a local story, then approach the person of interest about writing their story. (Caution them that you will only be pitching the story and it's not a big Hollywood movie.) If it's a national story, you may need an agent to secure the rights for you. If you don't have an agent, always have a lawyer draft a contract for you.

The other option is to do an "inspired by true events" story. That's where you would take an existing true story and change all the names and places. What you're left with is the theme and general plot. You must be careful not to use any of the original source material. It's always recommended to check with your agent or lawyer when writing these types of stories.

Once you have some idea about what genre you want to write in and a story idea, you can expand it into a script. Start small and work your way up.

The Logline

Loglines are a standard in the film and TV industry. When a producer asks you for the elevator pitch it usually starts with a killer, memorized logline.

LOGLINE: a concise summary that distills your idea into 1 or 2 sentences.

LOGLINE FORMULA: When [*inciting incident*] happens, [*the protagonist*] <u>acts</u> against [*the antagonist*].

In the rom-com logline, the antagonist is also the love interest:

> LOGLINE FORMULA: When [inciting incident] happens, [the protagonist] acts against [the antagonist/love interest].

Here's a rom-com example:

> When Santa's [*socially awkward daughter*] is in training to take over his job, she [*crashes the sleigh*] and loses her memory, but falls for a [*swarthy mechanic*] who offers to help her.

> **TIP**
> Practice saying it out loud.

Here's a thriller example:

> When [*patients die mysteriously*], a [*recovering drug-addicted nurse*] believes [*one of her coworkers*] is a killer.

You can rework the phrasing until you find an effective statement:

> A recovering drug-addicted nurse must keep her demons at bay as she tries to find the killer of one of her patients.

This longer version adds more stakes to the story:

> Fearful of losing her job, a recovering drug-addicted nurse with memory lapses is led to believe she has accidentally killed a patient and must find the murderer before more people die.

You can move phrases around in the sentence until you settle on the perfect combination.

- You don't need to give character names, but do use a powerful adjective to describe the protagonist.
- You don't need to mention the genre as the logline should reveal it with the content: if there's a murderer as a character, then we know it's a thriller. But you will also reveal your genre in your cover letter.

- Use a powerful verb. Your protagonist must always be taking some sort of action to solve the problem.

Now put your story idea into a logline. Try writing a few versions of it. It will never be perfect and may even change as your story progresses. Don't overthink it!

Logline samples can be found as movie descriptors on IMDb, Netflix, or just about anywhere that screens and reviews movies. Study them and see what tempts you to watch.

> **TIP**
> Keep it to one sentence.

Once you have your logline, pick the strongest idea, the one you're most likely to be excited about throughout the scriptwriting phase.

Using your logline:
- brainstorm the major beats of the story
- write down scene ideas
- include the beginning, middle, and end of your story

This is a plot-based approach to writing and ensures the story hits all the needed plot points and cliffhangers.

Here's my brainstorm, using the thriller logline example:
- The nurse discovers her patient has died but can't remember if she gave the patient her medication — did she cause her death?
- After another patient dies suspiciously, the nurse suspects a coworker of foul play.
- The nurse narrowly escapes a terrible accident — is someone trying to kill her?
- The nurse is accused of murder and arrested by a (sexy) detective.
- The nurse realizes she's being framed and finds the courage to fight back.
- The nurse finally proves that her coworker or husband or friend is the killer, clearing her name.

So, these steps are linear and fairly logical. Yes, you may need to start with just the plain old facts, but each of these moments can be expanded and may spark your imagination.

Three characters were mentioned in this list. Using logic, what other characters might you need?

- A husband or an ex-husband who left her because of her addiction?
- A family member who has stuck by her but now doubts her?
- A nurse or doctor who can also be a past love interest and a suspect?
- A sweet patient who becomes the next victim?

Now that you have expanded your story idea, let's dig in and create some details. It's tough to write a story without considering who the characters are.

Main characters

The protagonist and antagonist/love interest are your key characters.

- Who is your protagonist? Describe her. Write a short bio for her. What does she want? What does she need?
- Who is your antagonist/love interest/killer? Write a short bio for them — give them a strong motivation for their crime.
- Describe the 2-4 main characters in the story.

A character bio can be a short (100 words) or long (300 words) paragraph and uses adjectives to describe each character. Don't waste words describing them physically, stick to their personality traits. What are her fears and flaws? What are her dreams and needs? Add in some backstory that's important to the current situation. For example, my killer nurse could be described as a hard worker who lacks confidence and is fearful of slipping back into addiction. But as a nurse, she is compassionate and caring — and perhaps has a touch of naiveté that makes her too trusting.

It's important to make character decisions before you start plotting. The character traits lead to plot. If your protagonist is finished with love because of a bad experience, we need to know why in the story. This event is what propels her through the story and creates a need. It's also an element that pulls the audience in — we want the character to find love.

You have your logline and your characters. Now put it all into a synopsis.

The Synopsis

The synopsis is a short prose summary of the story, about 300–400 words. The story synopsis should concentrate on the protagonist — who she is and what her journey is. You don't need to include every character.

Your main character must have a complete journey or character arc:
- She should have an outer goal/journey: get the love interest or get the killer.
- She should have an inner goal/journey: discover her flaw and why it stops her from finding love or finding the courage to catch the killer.

Using only three short paragraphs, write a synopsis:
- **Paragraph 1** is the beginning of the story. Introduce the main character. We see where she starts and why she needs to change. (This is known as the character's ordinary world.) Something happens — an event that challenges her, makes her need to change, and propels her on her new journey.
- **Paragraph 2** is the middle of the story, her journey. What are the obstacles to her success? Does she have competition for someone's heart? Mention the stakes. What happens if she doesn't succeed — if she doesn't find love or doesn't find the killer?
- **Paragraph 3** is the wrap-up — the stunning conclusion. This is where it gets the most dangerous. If you're writing a thriller, then give us the darkest moment, the most dangerous event for the protagonist as she confronts the killer. If it's a love story, then show us that moment where the protagonist pushes love away, only to find it again. Include the ending.

Don't forget: You're telling a story — make it enchanting, exciting, romantic, moving, scary, whatever the tone of your story is.

Use language that reflects the tone and genre:
- Thriller: mysterious, dangerous, secret, deadly, obsessive, threatening.
- Rom-com: heart-warming, loving, sweet, rustic, romantic, love, love, *love!*

The Pitch Page

You've now completed the initial steps in your journey towards creating the script. The *pitch page*, or *one-page*, is an industry standard that all screenwriters use when pitching their projects.

> Title + logline + synopsis = the pitch page

The title, logline, and synopsis go together on one page. Writing a pitch page before you get to the longer materials accomplishes a couple of things.

It helps you narrow down your story concept and gives you an idea if there is enough material to expand.

The pitch page is also a touchstone as you take the journey through script development. If you get lost in plot details, you can refer back to it and see the bigger picture story.

In pitch pages, you always give the producer the ending to the story. Movie blurbs that you find on finished films are used to entice the viewer so don't give away the ending. The pitch page is also a sales pitch and should entice the reader/audience: the producer.

Here are the elements of the pitch page:

> *The Bad Nurse* (Use a catchy title. Thriller titles tend to be on-the-nose and often changed once a producer comes on board.)
>
> A TV Movie thriller (tell us the genre)
>
> By Roslyn Muir (tell us who you are)
>
> Logline: (one or two sentences)
>
> Synopsis: (three paragraphs)
>
> Contact info: (your name, phone number, and email and/or your agent's contact info)

Pitch Page Example

Here's the pitch page I wrote for the Lifetime thriller, *Stranger in the House*.

Stranger in the House

MOW Thriller by Roslyn Muir

Logline: Upon returning from her honeymoon, a lawyer, JADE, 30s, discovers that the caregiver she hired to look after her aging father has married him and taken over his life. When he's killed in an accident, Jade tries to prove he was murdered.

Synopsis: Up-and-coming lawyer, JADE ESPOSITO, 30s, returns from her honeymoon with new husband, MARCO ESPOSITO, 40s, a man she fell head over heels with and married after only one year of knowing him. But to her it feels right—Marco's her soul mate.

Jade discovers that while she was gone, caregiver SAMANTHA HARTLEY, 40, whom she hired to care for her ailing father, WAYNE GREGSON, 60s, has moved in and married him. Jade is disturbed by the new arrangement and decides to look into Samantha's background more closely.

Soon after, Wayne is killed in a car accident, and Jade discovers that the contents of her father's will were transferred to Samantha—who's now a rich woman. Jade sets out to prove that Samantha killed her father, but no one believes her—especially Marco who blocks her attempts to get at the truth.

She turns to old school crush and cop, LEVI DANIELS, 30s. He's a recent widower and just moved back to town. On Jade's insistence, Levi re-opens the case and discovers some inconsistencies in Samantha's story.

Jade sneaks into her father's house looking for evidence and is found by Samantha and threatened. Next morning, Levi is at Jade's door. Samantha is dead and all clues lead to Jade as the killer.

Jade manages to persuade Levi to give her twenty-four hours to prove her innocence. But what Jade finds is a sinister plot of revenge, and she's next in line for murder. She realizes almost too late that Marco is the murderer. She manages to turn the tables on him, and with Levi at her side, Marco is disarmed and arrested for the murders of Samantha and Wayne.

A year later, Jade has recovered from the grief of the deadly events, and she and Levi begin a new relationship.

Contact:
Your Name
Email
Phone Number

Before you get to the next step, you need to research whether your original story concept has already been made into a TV movie. Check Hallmark, Netflix, and Lifetime to see if there's anything similar.

It's heartbreaking to discover that your story isn't as original as you thought. But what better time to find out: after you have toiled over a 105-page script or when you have a one-page idea? Even if there is a movie out there with your exact concept, you can still twist that idea into something else.

> **NOTE**
> "I call dibs on this title!"
> Actually, titles can't be copyrighted. If you check IMDb, you'll see there are lots of duplicate titles.

You have your logline and synopsis but, before we get to the next stage, you need to understand the unique TV movie nine-act structure.

CHAPTER FIVE

The nine-act structure

You've honed the logline and synopsis, and your broad story points are falling into place. Before we create an outline and treatment, it helps to know the workings of the multi-act TV movie structure.

The format you must use when writing a TV movie is the nine-act structure, but how is this different from a feature film or TV series structure?

Feature films use the three-act structure.
TV series use varied structures depending on the network and/or streamer:
- Comedies tend to be a half-hour: Cold open and two or three acts.
- Dramas tend to be one hour: Cold open and four to six acts.

That's why there's always confusion: is a TV movie more like a feature film or a TV series? It's kinda both. But usually, a TV movie is a movie that wasn't released theatrically. It was created specifically for a TV audience.

Why are there such different act counts and formats? TV commercials.

Cable networks like Hallmark and Lifetime count on income from commercials. More commercials equals more income.

Streamers like Netflix count on subscriptions for income and the big draw is no commercials.

Over the years, TV movies have evolved from six acts to nine as the networks saw a way to increase the commercial breaks. The nine-act structure is built around their commercial breaks. When writing your TV movie, do not change this act structure.

A TV movie runs two hours with commercials.

All times are approximate and used primarily by Lifetime and Hallmark — other networks may vary. Even though Netflix and other streamers don't have commercial breaks, they still use the nine-act structure in their TV movies. It's partly because they are emulating the popular TV movie networks but also because it's a format that works.

> BROADCAST RUNNING TIME
> FOR TWO-HOUR FORMAT
> 9 acts/8 commercial breaks
>
> ACT 1 runs for 20:00
> *Commercial break 3:45*
> ACT 2 runs for 12:00
> *Commercial break 4:00*
> ACT 3 runs for 9:00
> *Commercial break 4:00*
> ACT 4 runs for 9:00
> *Commercial break 4:00*
> — MIDPOINT —
> ACT 5 runs for 8:00
> *Commercial break 4:00*
> ACT 6 runs for 7:30
> *Commercial break 4:15*
> ACT 7 runs for 7:30
> *Commercial break 4:15*
> ACT 8 runs for 7:00
> *Final commercial break 4:15*
> ACT 9 runs for 6:30

The nine-act structure

This is the general script structure used by thrillers, rom-coms, and other genres of TV movie.

Act One

This is usually the longest act and runs for around 20 minutes.

This act introduces the characters, themes, and the central conflict. We see the protagonist's ordinary world, what her life is like without love, and/or her unhappy existence.

The inciting incident comes very early. We need to know within the first couple of minutes (Scene 2/3) what the problem is for the protagonist. If it's a rom-com, we find out why she thinks she doesn't need love. If it's a thriller, we find out that the protagonist has a big problem — maybe she's married to a killer?

Complications start as early as Scene 3.

- In a rom-com, we must have the meet-cute.
- In the thriller, we must have a crime and meet the killer — even if it's not apparent yet who the killer is.

Like all the acts, it ends with a *cliffhanger* or *act out* designed to entice the viewer to return after the commercial break. The cliffhanger is the most important structural element in the TV movie. With the exception of the last act, each act must have a cliffhanger.

- In thrillers, each cliffhanger at the end of the act will escalate the danger to the protagonist and move her closer to solving the mystery.
- In a rom-com, each cliffhanger at the end of the act will escalate the love interest and emotional journey of the protagonist.

Act Two

This act runs for 12 minutes, outlines the complications, and boosts conflict between the protagonist and antagonist.

- In thrillers, the female protagonist is often discredited by others and begins to believe it herself.
- In rom-coms, the protagonist is still processing the feelings that have arisen from her meeting with Mr. Possibly Right.

Act Three

This act runs for 9 minutes and ups the dramatic conflict. And this is where the push-pull fun and games of the rom-com really ramp up. The protagonist and love interest will have some flirty meetings and be excited about seeing each other again. In the thriller, the protagonist is actively trying to solve the crime and trying to find allies in her difficult journey.

Act Four

This act runs for 9 minutes. This is the most dramatic, exciting act and ends with the strongest cliffhanger to ensure audiences return after the *hour break*.

This is the *midpoint*. By this time in the story, the viewer must be hooked or they'll switch the channel during the commercial break.

In a rom-com, the Act 4 cliffhanger should be super romantic or full of fireworks. This is the point where you think the protagonist is going to fall for the guy, but some big plot twist gets in the way. Keep the audience guessing as to what's going to happen, but also up, up, up the romance!

This act can also include an unexpected plot twist or revelation that the audience is privy to, but not the protagonist. This can be where the protagonist thinks she's in love or refuses the one she will end up with. It can also be that first kiss or almost kiss. Either way, ramp up the chemistry between the couple.

In a thriller, the Act 4 cliffhanger should give the viewer enough incentive to return after the commercial break, so amp up the danger for your protagonist. Create a problem that comes out of left field: the protagonist believes her husband is the killer, or the audience finds out who the killer is before the protagonist and knows how much danger she is in. It's the *oooh!* moment.

Act Five

This act runs for 8 minutes and ends with a cliffhanger. Acts 5–8 ramp up the tension between the protagonist and antagonist — it's a game of cat-and-mouse. Or in a rom-com, the protagonist is falling hard for the love interest, but many problems get in the way.

Act Six

This act runs for 7½ minutes and ends with a cliffhanger. More problems arise for the protagonist.

Act Seven

This act runs 7½ minutes and ends with a cliffhanger. Plot twists abound! The rom-com protagonist is seriously doubting if she can ever love again. The thriller protagonist has discovered something unexpected and realizes she's in mortal danger.

Act Eight

This act runs 7 minutes and a huge crisis normally occurs by the end. It's the lowest point for the protagonist in either genre — nothing is going her way.

- This is where our heroine finally confronts the antagonist and is in the most danger.
- This is where the lovelorn declare they can't possibly fall in love — it'll never work. The couple believe their differences are too huge to overcome.

At the end of this act, the audience will feel emotionally attached to the protagonist and be rooting for them — but happiness or safety seems impossible.

> **NOTE**
> For Christmas-themed movies, all problems must be resolved on or by Christmas Eve, so that Christmas day is a happy, perfect time. Just like in real life!

Act Nine

This act runs 6½ minutes. The climax — the highest dramatic point of the story — is where the protagonist wins over the antagonist. It's the final showdown.

This act ties up the story as the resolution is reached in the last two scenes. The story ends quickly. There is no long, drawn-out ending, just a quick glance at how the protagonist deals with the ordeal, how her life has changed.

There must always be a happy ending in a rom-com. The protagonist must declare her love for the suitor. In the thriller, the protagonist must triumph over evil and solve the mystery that has perplexed her. The C-plot also surfaces at the end. The handsome cop who helped our protagonist can now be seen as a part of her happy ending and offer hope for a new life going forward.

How long should a script be?

Even though the TV run time will be very specific, your script pages can go over that limit. Each script page represents a minute of screen time: 20 pages equals 20 minutes. The page count of your script should be a bit more than the broadcast times. It's okay to overwrite, because editors will always need extra footage to cut around. A producer will always have the last word on this as pages equal dollars.

> Your script page count should look something like this:
>
> | | |
> |---|---|
> | Act One: Pages 1–24 | Act Five: Pages 60–69 |
> | Act Two: Pages 25–38 | Act Six: Pages 70–79 |
> | Act Three: Pages 38–49 | Act Seven: Pages 80–88 |
> | Act Four: Pages 50–59 | Act Eight: Pages 89–97 |
> | — midpoint — | Act Nine: Pages 98–104 |

Your script should be between 96–105 pages — this is the sweet spot. If you've written a script over this page count, do not pitch this out until you've edited it to the appropriate page number.

The great thing about this exacting format is that it gives the writer an obvious plot structure. I love structure! Believe me, it's easier to build your plot around cliffhangers and act outs. The strict page count is kind of like the thick black lines of a coloring book — it's a guide. But what exactly do you write in each act?

CHAPTER SIX

The thriller plot

I love thrillers! I read them, I write them, but luckily, I don't live them. (I'm fine with my quiet desk job.) Thrillers give the viewer two hours of excitement, and I love a mystery that I can't solve until the very end. The more thrillers you watch, the more you will recognize that they all follow the same basic plot structure. When you create your own story, be sure to include everything on this list.

THE BASIC THRILLER PLOT STRUCTURE

- The story opens with an exciting, high-stakes scene where the protagonist is in ultimate danger. This teaser could be a flashback or flash-forward.
- The set up: the protagonist and the main characters are introduced. The protagonist often knows the antagonist but believes them to be good.
- A theme is introduced.
- The bestie: the protagonist must have a best friend/ally/ confidante to share their worries with.
- The protagonist has a big, high-stakes problem that puts their lives, and the lives of their loved ones, in danger.
- The protagonist reports the danger to the authorities, friends, or family members but is not believed.
- Other suspects in the crime/murder/mystery are introduced.

Writing a TV Movie

> - A series of plot twists and turns initiated by the antagonist increase the suspense and danger to the protagonist.
> - As other suspects are eliminated, the protagonist finally discovers who the antagonist is.
> - The protagonist is often the final victim of the antagonist and they are captured or imprisoned.
> - The final showdown: the meeting of the protagonist and antagonist. This is where the antagonist reveals why they did all the bad things.
> - Just when the protagonist appears to fail and is in mortal danger, they find the courage within themselves to beat the antagonist.
> - The protagonist wins and is stronger and wiser from their ordeal.
> - A moral or lesson related to the theme of the story is revealed.

As head writer and CEO of content, you have the option of playing your story open — we know who the antagonist is right away. Or you can keep the audience guessing. Most TV movies reveal the killer/stalker/antagonist by the end of Act 4.

The basic thriller plot fits into the nine-act structure of the TV movie. Here's how the plot of Netflix's highly popular *Secret Obsession*, written by Kraig Wenman and Peter Sullivan, unfolds. (There's an interview with Kraig in the Resources section.)

> LOGLINE: Recuperating from the trauma of a hit-and-run accident, Jennifer remains in danger as she returns to a life and a husband she doesn't remember.

Act One

OPENING IMAGE: Torrential rain pours down on a dimly lit street.

On a dark rainy night, a young woman, JENNIFER, 30s, drives down the street trying to escape someone who is pursuing her. At a deserted rest stop, she tries calling for help but the phone doesn't work. She's pursued inside but eludes the stalker. Once she gets back in her car, she finds she's being towed. She gets out of the car and runs. When she's struck by a car [inciting incident], Jennifer is injured and left for dead on the street. [The story starts with a bang — the protagonist is gravely injured and requires surgery.]

Jennifer's handsome husband, RUSSELL, 30s, rushes to the hospital, worried about her. Soon after, she awakens in the hospital but can't recall anything about the accident or even her husband — she has amnesia. Jennifer's distraught that she can't remember anything, but Russell declares his undying love for her.

In order to help her remember her past, he shows Jennifer photos of her life. Charming, he regales her with stories of their courtship. He also fills her in on recent events: her parents died tragically in a fire two years before. Jennifer is shocked by the revelations and believes all that Russell tells her. [The victim believes the antagonist.]

A suspect is introduced — a tough-looking MAN, 40s, in a red car who was at the scene of the accident. He appears suspicious when he brings flowers to the hospital for Jennifer, which Russell notices.

Meanwhile, obsessed workaholic detective, FRANK PAGE, 60s, who failed to find his own daughter's kidnapper [relevant backstory], begins to investigate Jennifer's accident. [Page becomes an ally/bestie to Jennifer even though they haven't met.] He interviews Russell, who appears to be very concerned about Jennifer. Page also interviews some of the people who found Jennifer on the road and finds out that a white truck may have been involved in the hit-and-run. Page declares the accident an attempted murder, even though his boss doesn't believe him.

CLIFFHANGER: Someone is trying to kill Jennifer!

Act Two

Russell nurses Jennifer through her recovery at the hospital and then she is released. She's visibly better but still has memory loss and difficulty walking. Russell takes her "home" to their secluded mountain estate. But she is haunted by incomplete memories from the rainy night of her accident. Jennifer feels terrible that she can't remember anything about her life with Russell, which seems idyllic.

Detective Page requests that Jennifer and Russell come to the police station for questioning and mentions something about a witness. Russell doesn't believe she's ready but agrees. Jennifer overhears part of the conversation, but Russell lies and says it was a work call. Russell also tells Jennifer that she quit her job and her friends are away. She has no one to reach out to.

The man in the red car arrives home and doesn't notice Russell nearby. Russell confronts him about being at the hospital.

CLIFFHANGER: Russell bludgeons him with a tire iron. [This is where we see Russell for who he really is — a killer.]

Act Three

During the night, Jennifer is awakened by a noise beyond the garden — although she can't clearly see what it is, we know it's Russell burying the body. Next morning, Russell makes an excuse about what he was up to. Things don't feel right to her and she realizes Russell's behavior is odd.

Detective Page is still looking into the case and finds Russell and Jennifer have not shown up for the appointment. He does a search for their address, but nothing comes up. Page goes to the hospital and asks NURSE MASTERS, 30s, for contact info. She gives him an address and tells him Jennifer hasn't replied to her calls for follow-up treatment.

When Jennifer studies the photos of her and Russell, she realizes they have been manipulated. She searches for info in his desk, but he comes home. [Jennifer remains an active protagonist, trying to solve the mystery on her own.]

CLIFFHANGER: Detective Page realizes the contact info is incorrect and, in consultation with another officer, discovers that no one at the hospital actually called Russell to tell him his wife was hurt. [The detective is putting the pieces of the puzzle together and his actions keep us ahead of the protagonist.]

Act Four

Jennifer and Russell get romantic, but she has a memory that scares her and can't go on. Russell loses his temper with her, frightens her. He gives up and goes to his office. On his laptop, we see that he has cameras on Jennifer at all times.

As Detective Page burns the midnight oil, he calls Nurse Masters and asks her to search the hospital video footage. She gets security to send a file and tells him that Russell identified Jennifer with a tattoo she has on her back — the letter A. He gets the footage that reveals Russell getting out of a white pickup truck.

Russell apologizes to Jennifer for his behavior from the night before. Detective Page is able to trace the tattoo and figure out Jennifer's maiden name.

CLIFFHANGER: Page finds Jennifer's family home in San Jose and makes a grisly discovery — her parents have been murdered!

MIDPOINT: Here, we realize the ultimate danger the protagonist is in. Russell is not just a killer, he's a psychopath.

Act Five

Jennifer has a terrifying nightmare. Someone is trying to kill her. We recognize the house as her parents' place. While Russell showers, she grabs his wallet from his jacket and hides it. She pretends everything is fine, but Russell recognizes she's suspicious of him. *Click.* He locks her inside the bedroom.

She finds her driver's license in his wallet, is able to pick the lock on the bedroom door, and escapes. She then hacks his computer and finds photos of her real husband. Her memories come flooding back.

Detective Page goes to Jennifer and Russell's workplace but finds they both left the company. He sees a photo of them and discovers that the man he met as Russell is really disgruntled employee and stalker Ryan Gaerity.

Jennifer knows she's in danger, but the wi-fi has been disabled so she has no way to call for help. She hobbles out of the house and stumbles into the garden where she sees the partially buried hand of the man Russell buried. Russell, who we now know is actually Ryan, returns home.

CLIFFHANGER: Ryan finds Jennifer in the garden and knocks her unconscious.

Act Six

Jennifer awakens tied to the bed and confronts Ryan, who ignores her. He leaves for supplies and runs into Nurse Masters. She tells him the detective is looking for him. Worried, Ryan races away. Meanwhile, Jennifer tries to escape again and hurts her already injured foot even more. Determined, she succeeds. She hobbles to the garage and finds her car. And her old phone. Suddenly, the garage door opens. Ryan is back. He pops the trunk and we see the real Russell dead in the back.

Jennifer races back up to the bedroom and pretends to be tied up. Just as Ryan goes to check her foot, the buzzer for the front gate goes. Detective Page arrives at their home to confront Ryan and save Jennifer. As he looks for Ryan, Jennifer races to find him and escape. But Ryan gets the better of Page and knocks him out. [Her only ally is now gone!]

Ryan grabs Jennifer and tortures her by hurting her ankle. She's got no choice but to promise him she'll stay in her room.

Ryan locks Page in their freezer. Jennifer tries to get cell service and finds a video of her and the real Russell. Ryan returns and ties her up again. Ryan tells Jennifer how he was in love with her for years. He reveals his deep-seated anger that she was married and never returned his love. We see in flashbacks how he watched her and resented Russell, and how he finally killed him and everyone who got in the way. Fate intervened in his favor when she got amnesia.

CLIFFHANGER: Disgusted, Jennifer bites him and he leaves. [Never expecting her to fight back, Ryan is starting to come unglued.]

Act Seven

As Detective Page is trying to get out of the freezer, Jennifer is able to knock a lighter and candle off the table. When Ryan returns, he picks up the candle but doesn't see the lighter. She plays up to him and says she wants to give their relationship a chance. He goes to get her a drink. She retrieves the lighter and is able to burn the rope that binds her.

Ryan returns with a drink and she whacks him with a vase and takes his keys, then locks him in the room. She falls down the stairs, hurting herself, and slowly hobbles away. Meanwhile, Detective Page is able to force his way out of the freezer.

CLIFFHANGER: Ryan kicks the locked door open and pursues Jennifer.

Act Eight

Jennifer escapes the house and Ryan, armed with a gun, chases her into the deep forest. [It's the final showdown between protagonist and antagonist.] Detective Page follows them out into the woods.

CLIFFHANGER: Jennifer fights back, but Ryan overpowers her.

Act Nine

Ryan has his gun pointed at Jennifer, but Detective Page disarms Ryan before he can shoot her. A fight ensues and Jennifer gets the gun. She shoots Ryan, but only wounds him in the arm. In a last-ditch effort to get the gun, Ryan sprints towards Jennifer. She fires another shot and kills Ryan. It's over. [The protagonist has defeated the antagonist.]

Months later, Detective Page has retired from the police force and has packed up the toys belonging to his daughter. He's ready to move on — saving Jennifer has given him a bit of redemption. [She was the daughter he could never save.]

Jennifer visits, still limping but better. He gives her a note from her late husband that he had found during the investigation. As she drives home to San Jose, she hears Russell's voice in her head. He narrates the note and tells her how much he loves her. Jennifer's been through a lot, but the drive signifies that she's pushing forward, ready to create a new life. [A somewhat happy ending.]

FINAL IMAGE: Jennifer drives down the road towards her future.

FADE OUT.

The plot of *Secret Obsession* is a bit different from other thrillers because the protagonist is held captive throughout the story. Thus, an ally like Detective

Page is needed to drive the plot forward, but the danger for the protagonist still builds and ensures that the audience lives vicariously through her.

All of the cliffhangers at the end of an act are big, dangerous moments or reveals that put the protagonist in further danger. When writing your thriller plot, use the basic plot structure as a guide and include powerful cliffhangers.

CHAPTER SEVEN
The rom-com plot

Who doesn't love curling up on the couch on a Sunday afternoon and watching a dependable, fun, love-filled story? Your beloved TV movies use the classic rom-com plot that has thrilled feature film viewers for decades. These basic details are needed when you plot out your story.

> **THE BASIC ROM-COM PLOT STRUCTURE**
>
> - Introduction: the audience will meet the two main characters, *i.e.*, the lovebirds, separately.
> - The protagonist must have a reason to fall in love.
> - The audience must like the love interest. You can have multiple love interests who must also be likable.
> - The bestie: the protagonist must have a best friend and/or sidekick. They need a confidante, someone to bounce ideas off.
> - The meet-cute: this is where our two lovebirds meet and sparks fly — even if the love interest is someone from the protagonist's past.
> - Falling in love: the couple find ways to be together that are either organic or staged by an outside force. Their chemistry develops and the relationship deepens.
> - Turning points: a conflict, misunderstanding, or plot twist forces them apart and threatens to end the relationship. It can be a series of events that keeps them apart.

> - Breakup: the couple can't overcome the differences between them and break apart.
> - Reconciliation: the happy ending! The couple overcome their differences, conflicts, and misunderstandings and declare their true love for each other. They live happily ever after.

These basic plot points can also be seen in the Lifetime rom-com movie, *Christmas Pen Pals*, written by Carley Smale (there's an interview with her in the Resources section). I love this movie because, as a writer who loves structure, the theme is constantly reinforced.

> LOGLINE: After being dumped by her boyfriend, a dating-app creator returns home for Christmas and signs up for the annual Christmas Cupid anonymous matchmaking event in the hopes of saving her dating app, but finds love instead.

Act One

OPENING IMAGE: Sunrise in Seattle, Christmas music plays.

HANNAH, 30s, lives in a high-tech apartment; her only communication seems to be with Google's Alexa. Her sister, LUCY, 30s, calls and we see the contrast between Hannah's sterile existence and Lucy's cozy, happy, small-town existence. [The small-town trope is huge in these movies! Have I said that enough?]

Lucy tries to persuade Hannah to come home for Christmas, but Hannah says she's too busy with work. Then Hannah gets an urgent message from Perfect Match, a dating-app company where she works. Her boss NAOMI, 40s, is furious that for three months in a row, the app has been declining in use. No one is using the app to fall in love anymore. Hannah argues that her algorithm is foolproof, but Naomi wonders if people prefer falling in love the old-fashioned way. Naomi wonders about "the spark" you feel when you meet the right one and questions whether Hannah feels it with JASON, 30s, the boyfriend she met through the app.

Naomi sends Hannah to find a solution — without algorithms. Determined, Hannah messages Jason in order to figure out this "spark" thing. Does she feel it? When she gets home, Alexa reads out a message from Jason — he breaks up with her by text. Undeterred, she tries calling her old dates, but accidentally calls her dad, TED, 70s. Hannah reluctantly agrees to go home for Christmas.

Hannah returns to her childhood home and finds it's not decorated for Christmas. Ted doesn't bother because he's alone, a widower. Hannah is worried about him but is more horrified to find that Ted's stopped buying coffee and cut off his wi-fi. How will she check her email?

In town, as Hannah is trying to find a signal for her phone, she enters Sam's Café. SAM, 30s, the handsome love interest, is Hannah's first love. And when they see each other, there's a spark! [Meet-cute!] But friction starts when Hannah criticizes Sam for not having wi-fi in the café. He argues that simple is better. [The romantic couple always start out as opposites.]

A little flustered from the encounter, she gets a text from Lucy. She and son MAX, 10, are on their way to the café. Hannah rushes outside and intercepts them. Although glad to see each other, Hannah chides Lucy for not warning her about Sam owning the café. They had an awkward breakup. Max tells her that he entered the Christmas Cupid, a letter-writing tradition that builds relationships. They arrange to meet after Hannah drops off letters for Dad at the post office.

At the post office, her old high school teacher, MARTHA, 60s, is behind the counter. She encourages Hannah to sign up for Christmas Cupid. Martha is Cupid and sets up who will write who. At first, Hannah is turned off by the idea, then it hits her — this could help her with Perfect Match. She agrees to try it — but for Dad.

Back at Dad's with the family, Hannah coerces Dad to try Christmas Cupid. He refuses at first, then Lucy turns the tables on Hannah — she needs to sign up.

CLIFFHANGER: Dad agrees to sign up but only if Hannah does. It's a deal!

Act Two

Back at the post office, Hannah and Ted sign up for Christmas Cupid. They learn the rules. The letters must be handwritten and anonymous. The letter exchange culminates in a Christmas Cupid Festival where everyone will learn the true identities of the letter writers. As Hannah fills in the form, she picks "Stardust" as her pen name and ticks the box: seeking love.

Back at home, Hannah is recording her Dad as she asks him questions about falling in love. It's research. Lucy shows up and reveals there are already letters in the mailbox. Hannah and Dad get their letters and there's also an invitation to a free skate at the local arena. There, they can meet potential letter writers.

Dad and Hannah open their letters. Hannah's letter is from "Hutch." Doubtful about the process, she criticizes the letter writer because he made a spelling mistake. Lucy tells her to chill, but Hannah can't hide her lack of enthusiasm.

At the skating rink, Hannah is on wobbly legs. Lucy and Max help her. They run into SUSAN, 60s, the mayor, who is friendly with Ted. Hannah waves them all off because she's slowing them down. As she wobbles alone, she loses control and skates into the hot chocolate stand where Sam serves drinks. [They will continue to run into each other.] He jokes that he never thought he'd see her on skates and is surprised she signed up for Christmas Cupid. She assures him it's only research for her dating app.

As Hannah rushes off, she trips and falls hard. Sam tries to help, but DANIEL, local handsome doctor, 35, rushes up and offers his hand first. Hannah and Daniel hit it off, and she wonders if he is Hutch. They are interrupted when high school friend, SARAH, 30s, joins them and appears smitten with Daniel. Sarah mentions she tried the Perfect Match app but that the match lacked "spark," but she's excited about Christmas Cupid! [Another love interest, Daniel, is introduced. There should always be competition for the protagonist's heart.]

CLIFFHANGER: Later at home, Hannah writes a letter to Hutch and opens up about how she's feeling. Things are different at home and she's not sure how to change it. Maybe Hutch could help? Hannah drops the letter in the mailbox.

Act Three

As Hannah waits by the front door, Naomi calls. The investors are threatening to pull out, and she needs a solution by the New Year. Hannah mentions Christmas Cupid and how it could help the business. A letter pops through the mail slot. Naomi persuades her to open the new letter. Hannah does and reads it to Naomi. Hutch persuades her to get a Christmas tree and really get into the Christmas spirit. Naomi is excited — Christmas Cupid could be the next best thing!

At the tree lot, Hannah runs into GREG, 30s, former high school friend and now successful realtor. He's also doing Christmas Cupid. [Another possible love interest for Hannah! There are often two who vie for the protagonist's heart.]

Hannah discovers the tree lot doesn't deliver so, treeless, she goes for a coffee at Sam's. Sam's employee, JULIE, 20, figures out he still has a thing for Hannah when she shows up.

CLIFFHANGER: Sam offers to help her get the tree. Hannah's relieved and accepts.

Act Four

Sam and Hannah have the tree up in the living room. They joke about the letter-writing and Hannah reveals that her match seems cute. Lucy, Max, and

Ted return home. He's moved by the surprise and they decide to have a tree-trimming that night. He invites Sam to stay.

Later, the tree is decorated. Lucy and husband, JOE, 30s, help Max with the star, and they look like a perfect happy little family. But Hannah gets emotional and runs out. Sam follows her.

Sam remembers that it was a tradition for Hannah's mom to put the star on the tree. Hannah's touched that he remembers and is comforted by his words. [The emotions between these two will ebb and flow.]

Next day, Hannah takes Max to the toy store and they run into Daniel who is there with LIZZY, 10, his niece. As they head off to look at toys, Daniel flirts with Hannah — maybe she's his Christmas pen pal?

Hannah goes to the post office and chats with Martha, who has found a yellowed news clipping about her grandparents and how they fell in love writing letters. Hannah's excited about the news because she knew little about her mom's parents. [This letter-writing theme connects so many threads!]

Back at home, Hannah is now excited about the letter-writing. She tells Lucy and Dad that her pen pal may be Daniel or even Greg. The tables have turned and now Dad seems down on the letters; he's not sure he's ready to date.

Another letter from Hutch comes through the door. In it is a map to find "Christmas treasure." Lucy goes with Hannah on the treasure hunt. The path leads to a snowy wood and a present — beautiful star-shaped earrings — tucked in a tree. Another note mentions Hannah's favorite book, *The Christmas Star*. Hannah realizes she just felt "the spark."

CLIFFHANGER: Whoever sent these earrings is her true love!

MIDPOINT: This ends on an "up" for Hannah. It's a hopeful and emotional moment. The audience is invested in her journey by this point. We want Hannah to find love! So, of course, we will return after the commercial break to see what happens.

Act Five

That same night, Hannah writes a letter of thanks for the earrings and rushes out to drop it at the post office. She then walks by Sam's Café and finds Sam still at work making Christmas cookies. He says running the café is a lot of work; she shares that her business is in jeopardy.

Hannah helps put icing on the cookies and, later, they share cookies and milk. They banter about the old and new. Hannah represents the new, albeit cold, world; Sam represents the slower, more grounded world. Sam realizes Hannah is falling for her pen pal and warns her to not get her hopes up.

Writing a TV Movie

This leads to her apologizing for pushing him away when her mom got sick [backstory]. He reminds her they were best friends, and Hannah gets a lump in her throat. She rushes away.

Next day at the post office, Hannah's impressed so many people are waiting for their letters — there's a lot of excitement and hope in town. Hannah runs into Sarah and they chat about their pen pal hopes: Hannah shares that she hopes it's Daniel. When Sarah shares that she hopes her pen pal is Sam, Hannah says she doesn't believe Sam is writing letters because he wasn't skating that night. She encourages Sarah to pursue Sam anyway. After Sarah leaves, Hannah feels odd. Does she still have feelings for Sam? [This is the internal doubt or confusion about love that the protagonist often feels.]

As Hannah walks down the main street in town, she spies Daniel in Winston's Bar and joins him for a drink. Just as he reveals he's been thinking about her, his beeper goes off and he's called to work, leaving Hannah intrigued. She hears a group of guys laughing loudly behind her and turns to find Sam out with his friends. She joins him for a drink.

They reminisce for a bit, then when they go to the bar for more drinks, the bartender rings a bell. Sam and Hannah are standing under the mistletoe. Peer pressure makes them kiss.

CLIFFHANGER: Both are surprised at the feelings they have. It was a great kiss! [In this act, the competition for Hannah's heart really ramps up!]

Act Six

Next morning at the café, assistant Julie discovers Hannah was making cookies with Sam. Then, emboldened by her previous conversation with Hannah, Sarah shows up and asks Sam out. Sam is surprised to hear that Hannah actually encouraged her. [This conversation happened *before* they kissed, so now there are cross-purposes going on. Julie also has a minor plotline and letter-writing boyfriend-to-be.]

Julie persuades Sam to say yes, which he does. Sarah is thrilled. Meanwhile, Hannah has asked Lucy for Mom's amazing pie recipe and she bakes it for Sam. When she arrives at the café and Julie tells her Sam has a date with Sarah, Hannah's not sure how she feels. She runs into Greg and they head out for a drink at Winston's. Faced with a long wait for a table, Sarah shouts them over and invites them to join her and Sam — who is not thrilled to have Hannah there. Hannah excuses herself and Sam follows — neither of them happy that the other is on a date.

CLIFFHANGER: The sexual tension rises! They have an argument and Hannah says she wants to be left alone. Sam declares that's what she always says and agrees to leave her alone. When he leaves, she has a sinking feeling. [The lovebirds always have a spat!]

Act Seven

At home, Hannah has ice cream with Dad and they discuss falling in love. She's falling for the Cupid, but is still upset about Sam. He advises her to choose with her heart, not her head.

Hannah wraps presents with Lucy and Max. Lucy confides that Daniel is interested in her. Max reminds them it's two days until the big reveal and Hannah must write her last Christmas Cupid letter.

At the café, Julie gives Sam the pie, but he tells her to throw it out. She declares that Sam is in love with Hannah and that he has to tell her. [Julie is Sam's confidante and sounding board.]

Hannah writes her last letter to Cupid and says how much the letters have meant to her. She will wear the star earrings so he can recognize her.

CLIFFHANGER: Cut to Sam reading the letter he's received from Cupid: he recognizes it. It's Hannah! [It doesn't always have to be the protagonist's moment.]

Act Eight

At the post office, Ted runs into Susan, the Mayor, and an old friend. They chat and Ted bravely invites her for Christmas dinner.

Hannah gets her final letter from Hutch and he declares how much this letter-writing has helped him. He says he'll be holding her favorite book, *The Christmas Star*, in his hands so she'll recognize him.

It's Christmas Eve night. Hannah gets ready for the big Cupid reveal at the festival.

She tells Lucy that she's glad Sam won't be there, but Lucy's not so sure about that.

At the dance, the townsfolk pair up: Ted finds Susan is his pen pal. Max and Lizzy pair up.

Sam looks dapper dressed in a suit. Julie is surprised to see him there. He tells her his pen pal is Hannah and he's excited to see her. But then he overhears Sarah say that Hannah and Daniel like each other. Sam loses his resolve and gives Daniel the book so Hannah will think it's him.

Hannah runs into Sam as he rushes away. He tells her to have a great life and she is crushed.

Daniel and Hannah meet, and it seems meant to be, but she's still feeling a bit doubtful. Then she spies Sarah all by herself. Her pen pal hasn't shown up.

Sam talks to Martha and asks why she paired him with Hannah. She replies that she knows true love when she sees it.

CLIFFHANGER: Sam leaves. [The lovebirds have given up on each other.]

Act Nine

Hannah and Daniel go for a walk outside in the snow, but their conversation seems forced. Hannah soon realizes that Daniel isn't her pen pal — he's Sarah's.

Back at home, Hannah is upset over Sam. She goes through her old letters from Sam in college and realizes that he and Hutch made the same spelling mistakes. Her pen pal is Sam! She starts writing a letter....

It's Christmas morning. Sam is in the café and reads the letter from Hannah, that she slipped through the door earlier on. Then Hannah arrives. He apologizes for not telling her he was taking part in the Christmas Cupid. They declare their love for each other. They kiss. Yes, the spark is there!

FINAL IMAGE: Christmas bells ring throughout the town. Merry Christmas!
FADE OUT.

Note the opening and closing images: we open on a big, cold city and end on the warm, inviting small town.

Did you count the Christmassy moments? Ice skating, tree-decorating, cookie-making, mistletoe-kissing, and a Christmas Eve dance are good examples of key thematic moments in this movie. All holiday rom-coms must have them and it's the writer's job to instill uniqueness in them. But even if you lifted the Christmas elements out of the story, the plot would still work as a rom-com or it could become a Valentine's Day story.

Hannah is an active protagonist and the love interest, Sam, plays a big role. The letter-writing theme is used throughout as almost every character, with the exception of Lucy, is in need of love. This is a complex plot!

All of the cliffhangers are emotional moments that tug at the heartstrings. We are meant to feel the push and pull of Hannah's journey to find love. Along the way, she has changed. She's no longer the big city girl who's cold and immune to love; by going back to her roots and becoming part of the town, she has found her true self and true love.

CHAPTER EIGHT
Writing the TV movie script

Now that you have a handle on the nine-act structure and the thriller and rom-com plots, it's time to write your script. Well, almost. Before you get to the script, I highly recommend you take the time to write an outline and a treatment. They both allow you to delve deeper into the story.

The Outline

The outline is a two- to three-page synopsis of the entire story. It expands the short synopsis you created for the pitch page and gives more details about the plot. This is where you can introduce the supporting characters and subplots.

It has the same style and tone as the synopsis and is also a sales-type document that producers will use when pitching the idea to a network.

A producer will often want to read a logline, a synopsis, and an outline or longer synopsis before even looking at the script. You can send the pitch page (one-sheet) or the outline, depending on what the producer requests. When a producer buys your script, they will use these materials to pitch to a network and distributor. So, the work you do before you write the script will not be in vain.

You can use an outline in a few ways:

- Use it to outline and develop your story in prose,
- Adjust any changes you have made during the writing process, or
- Polish it up and use it when requested after a pitch.

How to write an outline

Start your outline with nine sentences, each sentence representing an act. You can use details from your pitch page synopsis as well. Focus on the A-Plot — the mystery or romance. Add in all the cliffhangers for each act.

In a thriller, you will need to outline the crime and clue path that gets the protagonist to the final showdown with the villain. Make sure the intricacies of the crime work first, so you don't have to go back later and figure it all out.

> **THRILLER PLOTLINES**
> A-PLOT — Protagonist solves the mystery, 75%
> B-PLOT — Protagonist personal/relationship issues, 20%
> C-PLOT — Love story, 5%

In a rom-com, you will need to outline the love story that gets your protagonist to that final kiss. Don't worry about the minor characters at this point. Focus on the protagonist, what she needs and how she gets it. What are the obstacles that get in her way?

> **ROM-COM PLOTLINES**
> A-PLOT — Love Story, 75%
> B-PLOT — Protagonist personal/career issues, 20%
> C-PLOT — Seasonal problem, 5%

Once you have the A-Plot figured out, you can start adding in the subplots. Keep the outline at two to three pages single-spaced. Make the paragraphs short — no more than four to five sentences each. It needs to be readable but also compelling. Now write the outline!

> **TIP**
> Read it out loud to yourself or a friend. Make sure your plot makes sense, polish it up, and then start the treatment.

How to write a treatment

The treatment is usually ten to fifteen pages long. It's different from the outline, as the language changes. The synopsis and outlines are overviews of the story — you are describing the story. The treatment is more like the script, but without the dialogue.

I usually cut and paste my outline into my screenwriting software. Use act breaks and scene headings like you would in the script.

Here's a thriller example:

ACT ONE

INT. HOSPITAL - HALLWAY - NIGHT

A lone figure dressed in black slips down the dim hallway, unseen. A gloved hand settles on a door handle and quietly opens it.

INT. HOSPITAL - NURSES STATION - NIGHT

Dressed in blue scrubs, nurse GEMMA STILCHON, 33 brushes a strand of hair from her face as she fills in a patient chart. Gemma rubs her eyes, glances at the clock that reads 3:00 a.m.

A NOISE from down the hall catches her attention. She walks around the desk and looks down the long, dim hallway. Is someone there? After a moment, Gemma goes back to her desk and picks up the file.

Suddenly an alarm goes off. A blue light flashes above Gemma. She freezes.

Footsteps from behind. NURSE WILSON, 40s, rushes past her. CODE BLUE. Gemma comes to her senses and dashes after her coworker.

INT. HOSPITAL - PATIENT'S ROOM - NIGHT

Gemma and Nurse Wilson stand over a patient — now dead. As Gemma looks at her patient in disbelief, Nurse Wilson gives Gemma an accusatory look.

In this thriller example, the action starts right away — with the crime and our protagonist. Dive into the story and hook the reader as soon as possible. In three short scenes, we've set up the antagonist, the protagonist, and the circumstances — murder.

The viewer knows that Gemma is innocent because they saw the lone figure skulking down the hallway. That intimacy with the protagonist also helps the viewer care about her.

The beauty of writing a treatment for your script is that you're telling the entire story using action only. It allows you to take a deep dive into the plot without the dialogue getting in the way and explore the emotional arcs of the characters.

In both the thriller and the rom-com, the protagonist must have a compelling journey. They must have an inner and outer goal — and they must be successful. The protagonist's arc is the structural wall holding your script in place. This journey is more apparent in a treatment and it's easier to fix any problems in this shorter document.

The treatment is also used when working with producers, networks, and distributors. If you have pitched an idea and have not yet written the script, then they may want to approve the treatment before it goes to script. Some producers will send in a treatment before they send in the script. It's a quicker read and easier to give notes on the story.

In a treatment, you're also setting the tone and creating the locations for the story. Try to keep the locations to a minimum. This isn't a feature film with a huge world. In *Secret Obsession* and *Christmas Pen Pals*, the home was the key location. Rom-coms tend to have more locations because the protagonist is often in their hometown and interacts with many characters. Since thrillers tend to be lower budget, they take advantage of one key location like a home, hospital, or work environment.

Additional things to consider as you write your treatment

LOCATIONS: Use only three to five main locations in your story. Producers will love a script that mostly takes place in one or two houses.

CHARACTER NUMBERS: We've talked a lot about the main characters — the protagonist and antagonist. But how many other characters does your script need? In addition to the two main characters, you can have two more lead characters and two to four supporting characters. Overall, no more than ten characters with speaking roles. Background actors should be used sparingly. Allow for one or two crowd scenes and make them count.

At this point, you may be thinking — will structure make your script formulaic? Possibly. But you're responsible for the content, the unique story. Sticking to the formula the network uses not only makes the process cleaner and more efficient — it makes you a professional.

The script

You've done all the hard work. You have your pitch materials and your story treatment. Now it's time to expand that treatment into a screenplay. Add the dialogue, hone the moments, and keep an eye on the page count for each act. If you're in need of more inspiration, watch a couple more TV movies!

There are a few things to note before writing the script.

DRIVING SCENES: Do not write scenes between characters in moving cars. It's okay to have a character get into or out of their car after parking, but it adds substantially to the budget if the car has to be moving through a location.

AVOID STATIC SCENES: If your characters are just standing around chatting, add some action to the scene. Actors love to have something to do in a scene — it makes their performance more interesting. In a Christmas rom-com this is easy to solve — have them baking cookies, wrapping presents, or trimming the tree!

OVERALL SCENE COUNT: A producer will always have the last word on this, but a two-hour TV movie averages about 80 scenes. If your scene count comes in over that, look for places where you can merge scenes or change locations. Your screenwriting software can add in the scene numbers for your reference, but don't leave them in when sending the script to a producer. Limit the montages you have in your script as they usually include multiple locations and become expensive to shoot.

If you haven't written a screenplay before, I suggest you read several scripts, so you understand the expected format. Film and TV scripts can be found online and are downloadable, but unfortunately, it's very hard to find any TV movie scripts. There are also many great books on screenwriting available wherever you buy your books (see Resources).

Screenwriting software

Invest in professional software like Final Draft or Movie Magic Screenwriter. It makes your job easier. It supplies a TV movie template and shows the producer that you're a serious writer. Also, most producers will have these programs so that they can read the scripts and send notes to the writer.

Once you have sold a script to producers, they will ask you to submit the script in either Final Draft or Movie Magic Screenwriter formats that will enable them to break down the script for production. The software enables them to count characters in the script and see which characters occur in each scene. They use the character breakdowns to set the budget and do casting.

There are a few free screenwriting programs out there on the internet. You can use these when you're starting out. They're good for practice with the screenwriting format, and to see how invested you are in this screenwriting thing. However, they often have watermarks that show up when printing on paper or as a PDF. You should never submit watermarked scripts to producers — it screams newbie!

Twelve-point Courier font is the film and television industry standard. Do not change it. New writers often complain about the look of the font and how they prefer another, but it's the mark of a rookie if you hand in anything other than Courier. Producers are always looking for reasons to turn down a script or stop reading after one page — the font switch is an immediate red flag. Assume it will promptly be thrown in the trash.

Make sure you pick the "One-Hour TV Drama" format in your software. That way you can put in the act breaks. Some writers take out the act breaks when they send the script to producers, but some keep them in. You can ask your producer what they prefer.

During early development, I recommend using the act breaks to help you track the pages for each act. It also helps the producer when they are giving feedback to refer to each specific act.

Self-editing the script

Once you've finished the draft, leave it for a week or so and go brainstorm five other TV movie ideas and write the logline for each. You will want to have these in case a producer asks: *What else you got?*

But more importantly, giving yourself a break from the script makes you more objective when it's time to give it another pass.

Start with structure:
- Count out your pages for each act. Have you adhered to the page count?
- Is one act more heavily weighted?
- Does each act end with a cliffhanger?
- Is the midpoint obvious and enticing?

Content:
- Is your protagonist driving the action?
- Is the antagonist formidable?
- Is the love interest lovable?
- Do you have more than 2 crowd scenes and too many cast members?
- Check each scene heading and make sure they are consistent. Can you combine scenes into one location?
- Look at character names and ensure none of them start with the same initial, which can be confusing to the reader.

Never send out a first draft that no one has read or given you notes on. Always self-edit and then find someone with editing skills to read it for you.

Consider hiring an experienced story editor to give you notes on the draft. They will offer the bigger picture notes but can also give specific notes on dialogue, typos, etc. Yes, it's expensive to hire a professional editor, but you get honest feedback and pro notes.

Proofread

Once you're ready to send, find a reader to proof your work. Nothing turns off a producer more than a typo-filled script and they will stop reading it.

Reach out to writer friends and screenwriting groups to read your script for you. Don't have family members or friends who are not screenwriters read it. They usually don't understand the screenplay structure. But you can ask a trusted friend to proofread for you. Once your script is polished and you're sure the plot is exciting and intriguing, it's time to pitch it out.

PART THREE

Pitching your project to producers and next steps

CHAPTER NINE
How to find producers to pitch to

Back at the beginning of the book, I asked you to research the TV movies in the genre you'd like to write. Once you've done all the research and tracked the TV movie producers, you should have a list of producers. Search for them online. They will usually have a production company and a website where you can gather information.

You will often find many types of producers listed in the credits of movies and on production company websites: executive producer, producer, co-producer, or associate producer. The producers who make the decisions about scripts are usually those credited as producer or executive producer, depending on the size of the company. In smaller companies, often the producer wears many hats. Larger companies will often have producers or staff in charge of script development — those are the people to contact.

Check production company websites for any script submission details. If they say they don't take unsolicited submissions, then don't send them anything — it will just be deleted. Make sure that they produce the genre you're writing. If they only do Christmas movies, don't send them your thriller.

If your city, state, or province has any film production at all, then they probably have a film office or film commission. The film commission usually keeps an updated list on their website that tells you what is in production — they should also have a list of local producers and their companies. You can check out their websites or give them a call and ask them for a production company list.

> **TIP**
> Producers do like to hire local writers. Often, there are tax credits and production incentives they can access for using local talent.

The Pitching Process

Writers have long dreaded this crucial next step — pitching and sending out your work. You must learn to treat your writing like a business. Be bold. Producers want and need your product.

Yes, you can send multiple submissions to producers. If you sent it to one producer at a time, it would take years to get any responses.

Use a spreadsheet to track all the contacts you have made, the dates you pitched, and any follow-up emails you've sent. Make detailed notes — trust me on this.

There are a few ways to contact a producer and pitch your movie:
- By phone
- By email
- By personal referral

Most writers are pitching by email these days. *Whew!* Just what introverted writers want to hear! However, if you don't have a contact email for a producer, cold-calling the production company will be the best option. Now is the time to check out IMDbPro.com where you can get a free trial or buy a subscription and access film industry contact information.

The cold call

In order to get that in-person or online pitch meeting, you will need to contact the producer first and request a meeting. If you can't speak to a producer (make sure you have a name), an assistant may be able to help you. Be respectful of assistants: keep in mind that they may be assistants now, but they may be on their way to becoming producers someday. Also, they usually have the producer's ear (they were hired for a reason) and can end up being your advocate.

State your goal: Can you set up a pitch meeting with the producer? Ask questions — how do the producers like to be pitched? Can you email a treatment or a script or both? What genres are they looking for? Hopefully, your initial research will have shown that you're pitching your rom-com or thriller to the right producer. Usually when booking pitch meetings, the producer or assistant will ask you to send materials in advance.

The meeting

When you do get to meet the producer in person or chat on the phone, be prepared. Rehearse your logline so that it's conversational. Give them a short synopsis of the story. Don't try to tell every scene and detail — it's an overview. Make it exciting — enhance the mystery and stakes.

Expect questions. Take notes. And always go in with a few ideas for other TV movies. They don't have to be written scripts, but it shows that you're interested in the genre.

Producers want to work with nice people — be pleasant and excited about your script concept. If you're nervous, then write out a script and practice your responses to questions that might arise. Memorize your elevator pitch and frame it with casual conversation. Briefly, tell them a little bit about you and why you're compelled to tell this story. If you have humor in your arsenal, use it — even when selling a thriller.

If it's a phone meeting, don't take up too much of their valuable time. Be brief. Introduce yourself, tell them you've got a script, slip in the logline, and ask if you can send the materials for their consideration. Don't give a big spiel about the story unless asked to expand on the logline. The goal is to get them to read your script or pitch materials.

Show interest in their company and ask what they're looking for. Sometimes it's not apparent from the company website that they also do other genres.

If you have an agent, then they can also pitch your work for you and introduce you to producers. But if you're reading this book and writing your first TV movie, chances are you haven't yet found an agent.

If you do have email contact information for a producer, then use it first over a cold call.

> **Tip**
> The best time to approach an agent is when you have an imminent deal.

The email submission

Never send a script or any attachment in an introductory email. If a producer receives an email with an attachment from a person they don't know, they will delete it — unread. Besides the security issues, they won't want to read anything without a signed release form.

Send only a logline, the genre, and a brief synopsis in the body of the email. Unless you have specific instructions from a producer you've already spoken to, you only want to send an introductory message.

When emailing a producer, make sure that your letter is short and to the point. If you're not confident in your letter-writing skills, have someone proof it for you. There are plenty of online resources if you need help with a cover letter or email protocols. You only need one letter — you can reuse it.

Don't send it out as a form letter with "Dear Sir/Ma'am." That's a big turnoff for producers. Personalize your cover letter. Do your homework. Have you seen one of their films? Comment on them. Be genuine.

Here's a sample letter:

> Dear [producer name],
>
> I see you're a producer of Hallmark rom-coms. I enjoyed [insert title of their latest movie here] and would like to submit the rom-com script I have written. My first draft script is about a woman who [insert logline here].
>
> I've recently graduated from [insert school here] and my short film screened at several festivals including [insert film festivals here]. I think my TV movie, [*Title*], would fit well with your current slate.
>
> I'm happy to send a treatment or script at your request. Thanks for your consideration.
>
> Yours sincerely,
>
> Polite Writer.
> [add a link to your website, if any]

Briefly mention any pertinent credits you have. Talk about yourself. Even if you don't have any professional credits, you can find something to mention:
- any short films you might have made
- writing contests you've entered and done well in
- you're a recent film school grad
- you've had success in another genre
- you've published a book
- you have a successful career that relates to your script (for example, wedding planner, psychologist, lawyer, cop, doctor, etc.)

When to follow up

Two weeks is an appropriate time to follow up with any email queries, depending on what sort of correspondence you have had with the producer. If they've responded and replied to your email and would like to read your script or treatment, then you may have been given a target completion date already.

If you haven't heard any response whatsoever about your initial inquiry, let it go. If they don't return your email, they generally aren't interested. It's a blunt answer, but it may be all the busy producer can do.

Don't be offended — this is normal. Have you ever sent out resumés for a job and been told that only the shortlist will be contacted? It's a similar process in the film and TV industry.

Often a producer is in production on a movie and doesn't have time to read and consider your pitch. Or they are overwhelmed with other writers submitting to them and don't have the staff to respond. Or they don't take unsolicited material. Don't take it personally.

If the producer does request your script, you are free to keep submitting it to other producers until you have genuine interest and a contract on the table. Regardless of the circumstances, always be polite and businesslike.

Do not send a script that hasn't been edited or read by another writer or an editor. It's crucial that you know your script is pitch-ready. It must be error-free. I can't stress this enough.

Never drop by a production office and drop off an unsolicited script. It's a no-no. Most producers won't even take hard copy scripts anymore. You must send them by email as an attachment — and only at their request.

Don't burn any bridges! Staying professional with all of your contacts will have an impact. Even if they're not interested in your first, second, or third pitch, they may like something later on.

The personal referral

The film and TV industry thrive on personal referrals. Producers like it when someone can vouch for a new writer. If you know anyone who has worked for one of your target producers, ask for an introduction. This is the best way to get a meeting. It does take time to network and find these connections, but it isn't impossible. Likewise, if you have friends in the industry, you can pick their brain for contacts and get a referral. Don't forget to thank the contact that gave you the referral!

Signing an NDA

A non-disclosure agreement (NDA) is standard in the industry. It's primarily used by production companies to legally protect them. If they're already developing a story that's similar to yours — and yes, it happens all the time — then they are acknowledging that fact and making sure you understand it.

These submission documents are standard. Don't be afraid to sign them. If you have any concerns, you can always have a lawyer or agent look them over.

Online pitching options

There are many new opportunities to get recognition for your writing and sell your script online. Pitching on Twitter or other platforms is a way to get noticed by producers and agents alike. Writers have sold scripts this way.

Check out some of the online script platforms, such as Inktip.com and NetworkISA.org, where you can register your script and reach more producers. This is not an endorsement as I haven't used these platforms, but you can give them a try depending upon your budget as there is usually a fee associated with registration.

Whichever option you choose to pitch your script to producers, the important thing is to get your work out there!

CHAPTER TEN

Making the sale

As I mentioned earlier, getting an option or writing contract is the best time to approach agents. If they see you have a sale, they'll be more likely to sign you. They may relegate you to the assistant agent. Assistants are agents in training and are more driven to find new writers. If they like you and your work, you can work together and eventually they will be a full agent. The assistant agent will always have the more experienced agents check their contracts.

An agent who helps you vet a contract is under no obligation to take you on as a client, but it's more likely they will — especially if you have more scripts to sell.

If you're unable to find an agent who will help you with the contract, use an entertainment lawyer. Yes, you will have to pay for their services, but it's important to protect yourself. Never sign a contract without having a professional look at it and explain the fine print.

Shopping agreements

Producers may not want to option your story right away. Instead, they may ask you for a shopping agreement — a contract that locks up the script for a short period so they can shop it around to their distribution partners and funders to gauge interest. These are standard in the industry and unfortunately for the new writer, there is often no or low compensation.

Again, make sure you approach an agent or entertainment lawyer for advice on a shopping agreement. Keep the timeline of the agreement short. Opt for six months to a year, but don't allow any clauses to go beyond that. Some shopping agreements can bind the project for an additional year and stop you from approaching anyone they have already pitched — read the fine print.

The downside of these agreements is that once the project has a "no" from Hallmark, Lifetime or Netflix, there is often no going back to them with your project.

However, all is not lost. You can set aside the project for a year or so, write something else, then go back to the project and look at it with new eyes. If the producer gave you any feedback on why it was turned down, then incorporate it.

Shine it up, change the character names and even the script title — and recycle that baby! You can also use the script as a writing sample, so don't be afraid to send it around to other producers.

Always be truthful about the project's history: "Here's a sample of my work. It was shopped to Lifetime two years ago, but was a 'no'." A "no" doesn't mean that your writing wasn't good; sometimes they already have similar projects.

Producers will appreciate that you are honest about a script. If they read it as a sample and still think it has potential with a few changes, they may give you notes or take it further.

The screenplay option

When a producer offers you an option agreement, it means they are very interested in making your movie, but they need to legally secure the rights to do so. The option is a binding contract that will span at least two years and will come with an option fee. This fee can be anywhere from a symbolic one dollar to a higher amount.

If it's your first professional gig, you may not get an option fee — but if you haven't yet approached an agent for help, now is the time. An agent doesn't just read a contract and explain it to you — they negotiate your rate. They won't allow you to be taken advantage of.

The producer can't guarantee that your script will be made, but it stands a better chance now that they're invested in the story. The contract transfers the rights to them and allows them to pursue funding and partnerships. The option should also come with a writing contract.

The writing contract

TV movies are usually lower budget than a feature film or series, and producers don't often do paid development of the script, i.e., pay you for every draft you write. Producers generally want a sufficiently developed script that is almost production-ready — it just needs a polish and then it's good to go. But if they do want you to do a rewrite or polish draft, they should pay you for it. It's hard to estimate exactly what this fee will be as there are so many variables — what shape the draft is in, your writing experience, the country you live in, and your agent's ability to negotiate.

Generally, you will get a lump sum offer for the script and it will be paid out in drawdowns:
- A signing/option fee.
- A rewrite/polish fee.
- A production fee. The majority of the fee will be paid on the first day of principal photography.

Most productions will get the bulk of their funding when they go to camera on the movie and can't pay you until then. If you don't have an agent, you will most certainly be low-balled. Don't jump at the first offer. Instead, say you are currently in talks with an agent and you will run it by them. And you will.

Don't expect Writers Guild of America (WGA) or Writers Guild of Canada (WGC) rates on your first script, but do check their websites and educate yourself on their contracts and fees. Most TV movies are low-budget and producers can only hire non-union writers.

> **NOTE**
> If your producer loses their funding or distribution or something else happens and they don't shoot, you may not get paid. (Those details will be spelled out in your contract.)

As a new writer in the TV movie world, you will have better luck getting contracts with non-union producers who make a lot of product. As I mentioned early on — writing TV movies is an entry-level gig. Once writers have one or two movie credits, they will often look for higher-paying work, so there's always a need for new writers in this world.

Producers and networks are more likely to take a chance on a new writer without any credits — as long as your spec script adheres to the format I've presented here.

If you love writing TV movies, you can make a career out of it. With a good agent, you can build your rate and eventually get guild rates on your scripts.

Next steps

So, you've sold your script and your project is heading towards production. Congratulations!

But what happens next? Notes, of course. Yes, they bought your script because they loved it, but that doesn't mean it was perfect!

The key thing to keep in mind is that once you sell your script to a producer — it is theirs. They own it. Yes, you can disagree with their notes. But they now own the project, so if you want to continue writing the script, you will need to be open to their notes.

It's okay to push back a little — *my protagonist wouldn't do that*. But taking notes means creating a dialogue with the producers. You're both working towards the same thing — making the best movie possible.

Stay positive. The producer will hopefully have lots of production experience and their notes will improve the story.

Also, once a producer finds a writer they like to work with, they're more inclined to use those magic words: *What else you got?*

It's not only the producers who will give you notes. Producers have to answer to their funders — networks, streamers, and distributors. If the project gets the green light from Hallmark or Lifetime, then producers will get notes on the script from them. It's a high-pressure situation and the producer's career is on the line — if they want to keep making movies, they have to continually deliver on what was promised.

Once a director is on board, they will also have script notes. At this point, the notes are often to do with locations and making the script more visual and cinematic. Often, it's just logistics. "We don't have a staircase in the location." "Can you move this scene to the kitchen?" "Let's take this scene outside as we've been inside the house for too long."

Of course, the director's main job is to get great performances from the actors and to ensure the story is being told in its entirety. So, notes from a director may also focus on the emotional arc of the characters and plot.

As your movie goes into production, there may be daily requests for script changes. Scenes get cut and dialogue gets changed, deleted, or added. Often a director will just make the changes on set and the writer will not be consulted. Don't be offended if that happens. They're all working to make it better and have time constraints. And, time is money!

Depending on where you live, you may or may not be invited for a set visit. It's fun the first time and you always get fed, but after that, it's probably more useful to be sitting in front of your computer and working on new ideas. But do go if you're invited or needed. It's a chance to network some more with the producers and directors, which can lead to more work. If you love being on set (unlike me), then you'll find it very informative.

CHAPTER ELEVEN

Launching a screenwriting career

So, you've worked hard, written a spec script, pitched it out, and found a producer who loved it. Your script is in production, so fame and fortune are on their way!

Nope.

It might feel like that for a bit, so pop that bottle of bubbly and celebrate every win. Then get back to the list of brainstormed ideas and pick a new one to expand into a script.

Once you've written one TV movie, they do get easier to write. You will soon have a couple of movie credits and then you can start pitching ideas (not scripts) to the producers you have worked with.

Yes, producers can pitch ideas and get the go-ahead to develop them. But they tend to do that with writers that they know can deliver the script — fast. The turnaround can be up to six weeks.

Producers often have ideas of their own and will give an experienced writer a pitch page and hire them to write the script. They will also purchase good ideas — I've sold two pitch pages without writing the script.

Writing a TV movie is a way into the film industry and can be a continual source of income as you write that longer project and develop as a writer.

When you pitch your other projects, you will have renewed confidence and experience in the industry. Producers and directors will be more willing to read your scripts and to consider producing your work if you have credits.

All writing is hard work. Whether it's a TV movie, film, or TV series, you still have to show up on the page every day. Screenwriting is a marathon, not a race. That cliché exists because it's true. You're in this for the long haul.

All that is in your control is to hone your craft. Be better. Try new genres. Explore.

What else can a screenwriter do to help their career?

Join social media and cultivate a following.

Creating a network of film professionals is extremely useful. Every day, someone sees your posts and your photo. They come to feel like they know you. Make sure all your public media is appropriate for professional consumption.

There are tons of writing and filmmaking groups to join, perfect for the introverted writer who doesn't like to leave the house. Don't be that person who asks for a job. Don't message producers on social media unless they've put out a call for scripts. New producers often look for scripts via social media. I sold a script on Facebook that way. It really happens.

FACEBOOK GROUPS: While lots of individuals are ditching this platform, filmmakers and writers are big on it because it's an easy way to keep groups together. Join filmmaker and writer groups nationally and in your local area. Search for groups using terms like screenwriter, screenwriting, film & TV jobs, indie film, etc. Even if you're not looking for an on-set job, you can get to know the local players.

LINKEDIN: Cultivate a following and look up the producers on your research list. They are on LinkedIn and you should be too. You can post updates about yourself and articles you find interesting about screenwriting or filmmaking. You can also get contact information for producers and other filmmakers here.

TWITTER/INSTAGRAM: There are lots of people to follow and ways to stand out on these platforms, but it is time-consuming. Again, just be yourself.

TIKTOK/YOUTUBE: If you are also a filmmaker or just want to have some fun, then start making short videos. You never know who you'll run into.

Stick with a couple of platforms to begin with — I recommend Facebook and LinkedIn for professional contacts.

Social media sucks a lot of time and valuable energy. Don't give away your precious writing time by focusing too much on it, but do use it to your advantage. Make a rule that you will dedicate a small amount of time each day to posting on social media and stick to it. Reading articles or listening to podcasts about screenwriting is not an energy suck but can be inspiring. A good plan is to assign some of your available time to reading and research.

Volunteer your time and talents.

Is there a local film group that could use some organizational or creative help? Do they have events? Volunteering at film festivals is a great way to meet filmmakers and writers. You can also get free access to events, take part, and make contacts.

Most arts and film groups are nonprofit — could you run for the board of directors? All writers have mean note-taking skills that would be an asset in the boardroom. It's an opportunity to meet people in the industry — professionals and newcomers alike. The newbies you meet at these events could be working producers and directors in a few years. I can't stress enough how important networking is to a writer. The film industry is built on relationships — get out and make some!

Join a writing group or create your own.

Work on your art and don't be afraid to share it. If you cultivate a peer group, you may also hear of jobs and people who are taking pitches. It's a good way to get free feedback on your script and to learn to give constructive notes as well. Your understanding of the writing process will deepen, and you'll meet people who speak your unique language.

Be genuine.

Join and volunteer because you want to, not because you have to. But don't live in a vacuum. No one likes dust.

Believe in yourself.

Ultimately, producers are looking for people they can work with: *dependable writers who submit their scripts on time and are willing and able to take feedback*. This is the mark of a professional writer. Your only responsibility is to continue writing, work on your craft, create lots of ideas, and be prepared for opportunities — they are out there.

Good luck!

Resources

Question & Answer

I love to pick the brains of other screenwriters and hear how they got their start. Here's a Q&A with several successful screenwriters of TV movies produced for Lifetime, Hallmark, and Netflix.

Melissa Cassera
(Writer of the *Obsession* trilogy on Lifetime)

In addition to being a successful screenwriter with five produced films for the Lifetime Network, Melissa also has several TV and film projects in development. US-based, Melissa has over fifteen years of experience in marketing and publicity, as well as teaching courses in content marketing.

How did you start writing TV movies?

I didn't venture into a screenwriting career until my mid-30s. I'd run a successful marketing consultancy for over a decade and was used to storytelling through an advertising/publicity/marketing lens. For fun, and as an escape from work, I would write pieces of fiction and share them with friends. Eventually, I thought I'd give script writing a try and spent a few years learning and honing my craft through classes and working with a screenwriting consultant. Finally, when I had a few samples I was proud of, I just asked myself, "What kind of project would I want to make?" I'm a huge fan of Lifetime movies and really any "guilty-pleasure entertainment" like soap operas or angsty romances.

I specifically sought out people who wrote MOWs, produced them, directed them, etc., offering to buy them coffee to hear about their experiences. Through that, I eventually met a writer/producer who offered to read one of my scripts, then later became my mentor and connected me to my first job!

What sort of MOW genre is your favorite and why?
I love them all but, writing-wise, it's thrillers. My brain is a dark and twisted place. People joke that I'm like a fluffy unicorn on the outside and very disturbed on the inside — *ha!* I tend to be interested in the dark side of people, places, etc.

Has writing MOWs helped your career? How?
MOWs *are* my career. I absolutely love that in this space you have more agency, meaning most of the words you put on the page will actually show up in the final production. I also work with an amazing team of producers who allow me to weigh in on things like casting, editing, set design, etc. I get to be an influential part of the production. I also love the flexibility that writing MOWs provides. I lived in Los Angeles for five years while building my career, but really didn't like living there at all. Having a deal for MOWs provides the freedom to live outside of LA in a place I love while still maintaining a lucrative writing career, taking on other projects outside of writing when I feel like it, and to indulge in some other investment opportunities like real estate, art, etc.

What's your top tip for new writers wanting to write a MOW?
Watch a dozen of them and break them down, beat by beat. Get to know the structure, the twists and turns, etc. I'd also recommend only going this route if you're a fan of these kind of movies. It's very common for writers to assume MOWs are an easy paycheck and then end up getting fired off the project when they realize these can be just as (if not more) challenging than other projects. If you're a fan, you'll welcome the challenge!

Kraig Wenman
(Co-Writer of *Secret Obsession* on Netflix)
Kraig Wenman is a Canadian screenwriter of features and TV movies. He has 63 feature script sales and 27 produced films. *Secret Obsession* scored 40 million views in 28 days, resulting in one of the most watched Netflix Originals of all time.

How did you get into writing TV movies?
I started out optioning and selling features, and I got into TV movies by mistake. A producer had optioned one of my features and then the deal fell apart. The producer said, "We're not going to make it, but have you ever thought about writing TV?" So, it just came up that way.

I started working on an outline for a TV movie and learning the different writing style. I just figured it out because at the time there were no real resources out there and you don't learn it in writing school. When I started, I think it was 2005, they were writing in the seven-act structure, then two years later, it was eight then nine acts — to get more commercials in. I started watching TV movies and figuring out where the commercial breaks were, what the big moments were, the showdown between the protagonist and antagonist. I also directed music videos.

My wife said I could have time to write for a year, but at the end of the year I would have to work in her dad's car wash. So that was the motivation to treat writing as a job. I write from nine to noon every day, get my twenty pages done then I'm out. Sometimes I'll have two deadlines at the same time, so I'll write at night too.

I sold a lot of scripts on Inktip.com. That's how I made my first connections. I started optioning my scripts and got my manager and agents through there too. I sold about forty scripts through Inktip. They didn't all get made but they got me option fees. I was writing a script a month. Inktip also sends out a newsletter with posts for projects, so I responded to those.

Also, I found an agent and a manager through Inktip. Always have a contract before you approach anyone. Cold-call smaller agencies. Don't call William Morris. Find a small agency with one person. Or call and ask for a junior agent. If you have a top placement in a screenplay competition like the Nichol or Page, then that's a good time to approach an agent. You can also move up to a bigger agent, if you take an option contract to them.

What genres do you write?

My brand is popcorn with an edge. I like thrillers, crime thrillers, action thrillers. All based on MOW structure, but bigger films now. Someone has to die in the first page of anything I write!

I divide my time between writing, pitching, and brainstorming. I'll come up with a Hallmark pitch or a Lifetime pitch, or my agents are pitching me. I'll send out a logline then they'll ask to see a pitch page. I now go directly to the executive at Lifetime, Hallmark, or Netflix and give them four or five loglines. I give them options: If they say no to one, they might say yes to another. I'll often do a straight brainstorm day where I come up with twenty-five ideas then narrow it down to the best ones.

*You have a new Netflix movie (*Bandit*) going into production. Has writing TV movies changed your other writing?*

All my features are still in the nine-act structure. It's just better; something's happening every ten pages. The structure fits in a three-act, but it just gives you a twist every ten pages. Every ten pages, you have a fist come out and punch the reader in the face!

What are your best tips for writers?
I would say study the best thrillers of all time (they don't have to be TV movies) and check out the loglines on IMDb. Use these thrillers as inspiration and see if you can put a new twist on them. If it's *Misery* in a house, could it be *Misery* on a plane? What's a new twist in the modern age on the old stalker story? Change the viewpoint: now it's told by the stalker's point of view. *Rear Window* and *Misery* are movies I'm obsessed with and inspired by.

Look at MOWs, for example the stolen baby trope — how can you put a new twist on it? Check out the news headlines — what's scaring people today? Study the themes in the headlines. Gun control. Mass shooting. What's scaring the masses? Look to what scares you and what scares other people and examine the common themes.

Producers are always looking for true crime. It's better if you get the life rights or you take part of the story and say "inspired by". The only problem with that is everyone is going to be pitching what's in the headlines, so you have to find a new twist on it. Watch true-crime documentaries like *Forensic Files* for your clue path. Always figure out the crime first. That way, you can reverse engineer all the clues into the story.

Your first TV movies should be low-budget, about a million. Use only two houses in the story, for example. Big idea, small movie, as they say. The lead should be female and will always triumph at the end.

Write. Hustle. Every day. Get up in the morning and set page limits for yourself. Treat it as a job. There are a million reasons not to do something. Just do it. You can't edit a blank page. Don't be afraid to fail.

Don't think your idea is the best. Separate the ego so when you get the notes from producers, you can accept them. Beginning writers especially — you have to take the notes. Producers just want people they can hang out with. Pick your battles. The ego is the hardest thing for writers. It's show business. It's a collaborative art. You're an employee if you're a writer.

Carley Smale
(Writer of *Christmas Pen Pals* on Lifetime)
Carley Smale grew up in Peterborough, Canada, where she was an avid and obsessive movie watcher. At the age of 19, she moved to Toronto to attend the Film and Media degree program at Humber College. She specialized in

screenwriting and upon graduating, was hired as a development associate at a small production company. Eventually, Carley went on to pursue screenwriting full-time and has been represented by Integral Artists since 2016.

How did you start writing TV movies?
During film school, I interned at a small production company in Toronto that made TV movies — mostly Christmas movies and thrillers. I started out reading coverage and being an overall assistant. After I graduated, they hired me on full-time to continue being an assistant, but I decided to start writing treatments on my own and submitting them to my boss. At first, I think he was a little annoyed, but eventually recognized that my ideas weren't too bad. When one of them eventually sold, I went from assistant to one of the directors of development. I was soon given the opportunity to write the first draft of a Christmas movie called *The Christmas Parade*, and that's how I got my first writing credit. I worked there for almost three years before I quit to pursue screenwriting full-time.

What sort of MOW genre is your favorite and why?
I am definitely all about the rom-coms. They are essentially all I write. The most lucrative area for me has been Christmas rom-coms, but I am starting to get into writing summer/fall rom-coms too. I really love it. I am definitely interested in diving into thrillers at some point and more edgy content, but I am very happy in the rom-com space.

Has writing MOWs helped your career? How?
Writing MOWs is my whole career so I would say yes, *ha-ha!* I have an incredible agent who connects me with producers from all over and I've been fortunate enough to write for Hallmark, Lifetime, and even Netflix because of those connections. Of course, I fantasize about seeing a movie I've written up on the big screen, but with how much the industry is changing, that might not be a realistic goal anymore and that's okay. Streaming services are opening up a lot of doors for writers to try new things and it's really exciting.

What's your top tip for new writers wanting to write a MOW?
I would say watch a bunch of them. Note the ones you enjoyed and the ones you didn't and go from there. When I quit my job to pursue writing full-time, I spent a year writing two Christmas MOWs that I thought were both supercute concepts and also something I would actually watch. They both ended up

selling (*Snowed-Inn Christmas* and *Christmas Pen Pals*). I tried to give my characters witty dialogue in order to give the movie a more energetic feel. A lot of these movies can feel really expositional, which gives the characters very little personality and also makes the movie feel dull. Try to surprise the audience without straying too far from the formula.

Keith Shaw
(Writer of *Maternal Instinct* for Lifetime)

Keith is a producer and screenwriter known for the SYFY hit, *Malibu Shark Attack*, as well as many Lifetime thrillers. He's also been an executive producer on films *Absolute Deception*, starring Cuba Gooding Jr., and *Hard Drive* with John Cusack. He has taught screenwriting at film schools in Vancouver, Canada and Shanghai, China.

How did you get your start in MOWs?
I started working in documentaries as I have a history degree. Then I was working for a company that had bought the assets of a failed video game company. It was proving really expensive to reuse the footage and then I said, half-joking, let's use it in a movie. But then they said, "Okay, so how about you write it?" I said yes, and we went from that movie to female-protagonist kinds of thrillers and Lifetime movies.

What tips do you have for new writers?
Have lots of ideas. If you want to make a living at it, you have to have ideas. If you have just one idea it's tough, but if you have five ideas, one of them is probably going to resonate with somebody.

Do a sample script to prove that you can write and then it's the legwork of pitching. After a couple of scripts, you get a bit of clout. Even for directors, it's a good way to go — producers will give you a chance at directing.

A one-page is really all you need, and a script. Producers may like the idea you pitch and not like the script. They may give you notes.

As a producer, often first-time writers won't give back what I've asked for. I've given them notes, but they haven't done them. So, writers really have to listen and say yes. Say yes to almost anything! If they want a character or gender change — anything — say yes. Just get in the door. Go to the wrap party and introduce yourself to everyone. Network.

Go to AFM (the American Film Market in LA) at least once. You'll realize you're part of this big industry. It opens your eyes. You're not just sitting alone in your room writing — there is a huge industry out there. Contact the producers before you get there and tell them you're going to attend AFM, especially if you're from outside LA. You don't even need to have a ticket as most of the meetings are all outside. Or go to Santa Monica and just hang out. The MOW producers will meet with you. A couple of my screenwriting students went and they made unique pitch cards about the size of a playing card. They were like a big business card with their contact info on front and the script loglines on the back. They were very popular. So, find unique ideas to get attention.

I think your first job is often not your own script. Often, producers that you pitch have their own ideas and may ask you to write that.

Christmas rom-coms almost always get read by producers because everybody's looking for them. January is a good time to pitch them. Christmas movies don't necessarily need to be rom-coms — they can be a family story or the magic of Christmas.

A lot of people get the Lifetime thriller female protagonist wrong. There's no relationship — she's tough is all her character is. There's *always* a relationship in these movies — it's not just a tough woman on her own. Remember who the audience is. Women are there to watch 85 minutes of a woman in peril, then in the last five minutes she can beat up the villain. You can even have a rom-com in the middle of the thriller. Lifetime also likes to see movies that a mother and teen daughter can watch together, so try writing a script with a teen protagonist.

Put in a teaser at the beginning. The script is meant to be read — the first ten pages are the most important, so start big.

Kelly Peters & Amy Taylor
(Writers of *A Taste of Christmas* on Lifetime)

Amy Taylor and Kelly Peters have a very "womantic" story. They both attended the USC film program, but never knew each other at the time. Then they spent ten years in the same writers' group, evaluating each other's work, before they finally realized — "It's always been you" — and decided to pair up as a dynamic writing duo.

Since 2019, they've had fourteen features produced including the Lifetime thriller *Deadly Dating Game* and the Lifetime romantic comedies *A Taste of Christmas, The Dating List, Designed with Love, Heart of the Manor,* and *The Baby Proposal.* They currently have additional projects in various stages of development with Sunshine Pictures, Dawn's Light, Hallmark, and Reel One.

How did you start writing TV movies?

KELLY: Amy worked as lead writer at Hallmark's online platform Feeln (Hallmark Movies Now). One of the producers there moved on to another company that wanted to expand their regular slate of TV thrillers to include rom-coms as well. Shortly after that, we started writing a horror movie together, so when Amy was offered the chance to write more for that company it was a no-brainer for us to work together on those as well.

What sort of MOW genre is your favorite and why?

AMY: I have never had a favorite genre and instead have always responded to individual stories and characters. The same holds for MOWs. I respond to characters facing difficult obstacles and whose challenges allow me to see the world differently than I have before. I love the big escalations of thrillers and the cheeky banter of rom-coms equally — as long as they are connected to a character's inner life in a way that is compelling.

KELLY: Horror has always been my first love, but I also write historical romance novels and I've really developed a soft spot for MOW rom-coms. The dialogue is a lot of fun to write and I feel like I can channel my inner Rosalind Russell or Jane Russell (any Ms. Russell, apparently?). They're also more relatable. Most everybody falls in love at some point, but fortunately not everybody is stalked by their husband's psycho ex-girlfriend intent on stealing their baby.

Why co-writing?

AMY: We like to say we have a very wo-mantic story. We were both at USC at the same time but didn't know each other until we wound up in the same writers' group awhile later. We spent ten years in the group, reading and helping each other with spec projects. Kelly has always loved horror, so when some producers Amy knew wanted to make a horror movie, it seemed natural that we work together to write it. We not only had a great time but produced a great script faster than either of us could have done alone.

Co-writing definitely works for us but finding the right person makes a huge difference in the experience. We're well-matched in that we're both passionate and driven (both Scorpios!). We also have the same work ethic and commitment to projects so neither of us winds up feeling like they're carrying a project alone. At the same time, we also have complementary skills. Amy is a rock star networker, always on the hunt for new ideas and is great about finding little moments that make a story shine. Kelly has a phenomenal sense of structure, has the focus to bang out first drafts in record time, and keeps the financial side of things organized and up-to-date.

Our process can vary depending on the project, but usually we discuss the broad story together, throwing out ideas for theme, characters, their flaws, the setting, set pieces, etc. Then one of us will write up a 2–3-page pitch for the other to review. From there, we discuss more in detail on a long phone call. One of us will take all that and turn it into a 12–15-page treatment. Again, we review and discuss. Then one person goes off and writes the first draft, consulting with the other if questions come up or something's not working. Another round of review and discussions. From there, we pass the next drafts off as schedule and enthusiasm dictate. When you're on the fifth round of producer notes and your eyes cross every time you think of the script, it's such a relief to pass the next set of revisions to someone who can still look at the story with fresh eyes!

Has writing MOWs helped your career? How?
KELLY: Definitely! We've been able to establish ourselves as smart, reliable, versatile writers who understand the needs of our producers. And that's what every producer wants no matter what kind of TV or movies they're making.

What's your top tip for new writers wanting to write a MOW?
AMY: If you're looking to break in with a MOW, the biggest thing is to really understand the elements of your MOW genre. This isn't a time to try something radical or a big departure. For instance, the MOW romantic comedy genre calls for happy endings, flirty dialogue, romantic settings, and lighter themes. MOW thrillers also have happy endings for the protagonist, but also need significant thriller beats at regular intervals, and an early sense of danger or threat to the main character. The themes are darker (revenge, obsession, jealousy), but not superdark (incest, genocide, sadism). It's also important to keep production in mind since these movies aren't shot on summer blockbuster budgets. Limiting stunts, locations, the number of speaking parts, crowd scenes, and special effects will go a long way to helping a producer say yes to a well-written MOW script. Also, if you want to break into the business, let your fingers do the walking. Call people. Reach out. Don't be afraid to be a nuisance. Advocate for yourself and your writing and others will respond.

Glossary

ANTAGONIST
An adversary, foe, nemesis, rival, or opponent; the character who causes the most conflict for the protagonist.

A-STORY or A-PLOT
The main plotline in the story.

BEATS
A beat is a single unit of measurement of the action in a script or story.

BEAT SHEET
A beat sheet is a type of outline, a chronological list of all the points of action in a script or story. It's shorthand for the story, just the action.

B-STORY or B-PLOT
The secondary plotline in the story.

CHARACTER ARC
The journey a protagonist or any major character takes over the course of a story. The arc maps their *inner* transformation as they progress.

CLIMAX
The highest point of dramatic action/tension in the story.

CONFLICT
It's the external opposing forces between characters in a story. Conflict is internal as well — your characters must have inner turmoil.

C-STORY or C-PLOT
A minor plotline through the story.

DEVELOPMENT
The stage of script creation with or without a producer.

GENRE
The type or category of a story.

INCITING INCIDENT
It's an event or incident that propels the protagonist into the story. It's a problem that arises and changes the course of their life. It makes them question their Ordinary World.

LOGLINE
A concise summary that distills your idea into one or two sentences.

MONTAGE
A montage is a group of scenes that are thematically grouped together to convey the passage of time or condense events.

NON-DISCLOSURE AGREEMENT (NDA)
A legal document a writer signs when pitching a story to a producer. It protects a producer, especially if

they have a similar project already in development.

ORDINARY WORLD
It's the protagonist's normal life at the start of the story, before everything has to change.

OUTLINE
An expanded synopsis of your script. Does not include dialogue or scene headings.

PITCH
The act of communicating your idea to a producer.

PITCH PAGE
The one-page logline and synopsis of your movie.

PROTAGONIST
The protagonist is the main character in the story. The one person who has the biggest arc and who the audience follows throughout her journey.

THEME
The theme is the main idea or underlying idea of a story. It can also be the message of the story.

TREATMENT
A treatment is an extended prose telling of the story without any dialogue. It usually has sluglines identifying the locations and can run to about ten to twelve pages or more.

TROPES
Commonly recurring plot devices and clichés.

Recommended reading

There are many great screenwriting books out in the world. I constantly read and re-read my favorites for inspiration. Here are a few:

Save the Cat
  by Blake Snyder
This is my go-to book for writing feature film scripts, and there are many other versions of the book. It offers a unique, fun take on the traditional screenplay structure.

Screenplay: The Foundations of Screenwriting
  by Syd Field
This book is a classic and though specific to feature film writing, it spells out all the rules of screenwriting.

The Coffee Break Screenwriter: Writing Your Script Ten Minutes at a Time
  by Pilar Alessandra
This book is excellent for those who just don't have a lot of time to write. Her approach is to break down the writing process into smaller increments that add up over time.

The Dreaded Curse: Screenplay Formatting for Film & Television
  by Kat Montagu
This is a fun, easy-to-read book on screenplay formatting and a useful resource when writing. It's perfect for new writers!

The Idea: The Seven Elements of a Viable Story for Screen, Stage, or Fiction
  by Erik Bork
If you're stuck at the idea phase, this book takes a deep dive into choosing the right concept.

The Writer's Journey
  by Christopher Vogler
This is a classic for screenwriters who want to go deeper into story and mythical structure.

Writing the Romantic Comedy
  by Billy Mernit
If romance is your thing, this book is an excellent read. Primarily, it's about writing the feature rom-com, but there are lots of takeaways for TV movie rom-coms.

Websites

melissacassera.com
amykatherinetaylor.com
kellylynnpeters.com

About the Author

Roslyn Muir is an award-winning screenwriter and novelist who writes thrillers, family drama, and young adult fiction. Her TV movies have aired around the world: *Washed Away*, *Stranger in the House*, *Reluctant Witness*, *A Wife's Suspicion*, *Driven Underground*, and *Anatomy of Deception*. She was a writer on the Global/CBS one-hour drama, *Ransom*, created by Frank Spotnitz (*Man in the High Castle*). Roslyn also wrote and produced the dramatic feature film, *The Birdwatcher*, available on Amazon Prime. She has several optioned TV series.

Roslyn has an MFA in Creative Writing from the University of British Columbia, where she has also been an adjunct professor in screenwriting. She teaches film and TV writing at film schools in Vancouver, BC, Canada.

Her debut fiction novel — a middle-grade fantasy adventure, *The Chimera's Apprentice* — is also available on Amazon and other major retailers or at roslynmuir.com.

---

www.instagram.com/rosmuir/
twitter.com/rosmuir
facebook.com/roslynmuirauthor

For more resources and links, join my newsletter at Roslynmuir.com.

Made in United States
Troutdale, OR
04/22/2024